SURREY NATURE WALKS

David Weller

COUNTRYSIDE BOOKS

NEWBURY, BERKSHIRE

COUNTRYSIDE BOOKS
3 Catherine Road
Newbury, Berkshire

To view our complete range of books,
please visit us at
www.countrysidebooks.co.uk

ISBN 1 85306 610 9

Designed by Graham Whiteman
Maps and photographs by the author
Line illustrations by Trevor Yorke

Produced through MRM Associates Ltd., Reading
Typeset by Techniset Typesetters, Newton-le-Willows
Printed by J. W. Arrowsmith Ltd., Bristol

Contents

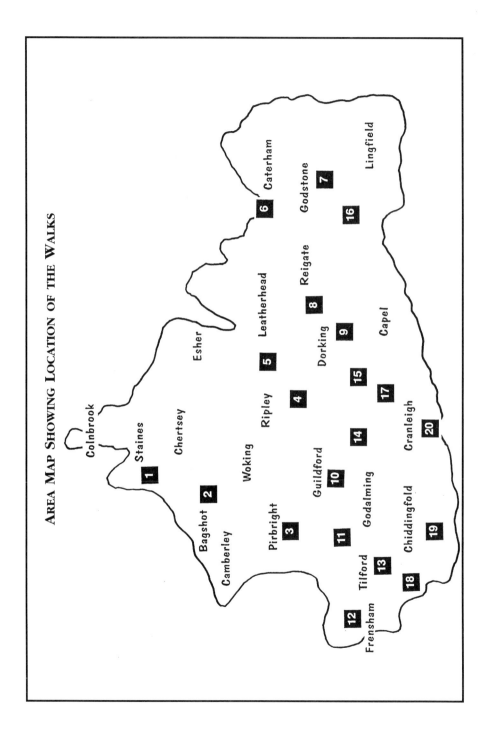

AREA MAP SHOWING LOCATION OF THE WALKS

Walk

PUBLISHER'S NOTE

We hope that you obtain considerable enjoyment from this book; great care has been taken in its preparation. Although at the time of publication all routes followed public rights of way or permitted paths, diversion orders can be made and permissions withdrawn.

We cannot of course be held responsible for such diversion orders and any inaccuracies in the text which result from these or any other changes to the routes nor any damage which might result from walkers trespassing on private property. We are anxious though that all details covering the walks are kept up to date and would therefore welcome information from readers which would be relevant to future editions.

INTRODUCTION

Surrey is one of England's smaller counties and fortunately for us also one of the most varied and appealing. Unlike Kent, the county never became 'the garden of England' due mainly to its poor soils and so was saved from the early plough. Large tracts of the forest that covered the weald were preserved for the Tudor kings and their courtiers to hunt the deer that roamed here. Surrey also became the preserve of the aristocracy who built large houses on their estates and in at least one instance even moved a local village into an unseen valley. By the 16th century, industries such as glass, iron and gunpowder developed in Surrey where the forest provided an ample supply of charcoal and water power. With these industries came the rich furnace owners and merchants who themselves built large houses, some of which survive today.

A century later, one of the most influential of these families were the Evelyns of Wotton. John Evelyn, the famous diarist and grandson of the original estate owner, did much to change the landscape around his domain. In repairing the extensive damage done to the woodland by these industries he took it upon himself to re-plant the northern slopes of Leith Hill with many thousands of trees. Fashion of the day dictated that he also create a contrived parkland scenery in the vale by his home. Not far away on the grassy sheepwalk slopes above Mickleham at Norbury Park it was recorded that forty thousand walnut trees had been planted. By now large areas of Surrey were being re-modelled by these great landowners and very little of its earlier scenery remained.

In other areas the exploitation of woodland continued until the once great forest had all but disappeared. The thinner and poorer soils to the west of the county could not recover from this onslaught and so our heathlands were born. The early industries have now gone, but to some extent Surrey is still used for the pleasuring of Londoners as the stockbroker belt testifies. This history of continual change to the landscape has led to the county's flora and fauna having many interesting and wildly contrasting habitats.

These lovely walks lead you through indigenous woodland, chalk downland, farmland, heath, wetland pool, watermeadow and along canal banks. Throughout the seasons these habitats have their own particular uniqueness whether it is orchids on rolling chalk downland in spring, dragonflies hovering above a wetland bog in summer, fungi pushing their way up through autumnal leaf litter in a beech wood or a flock of over wintering fieldfares on farmland. It is due to this great diversity that I have included a 'nature notes' section for each ramble which will hopefully provide you with a little more information on some of the things that you will see along each route. Please always respect the wildlife and do not pick any wild flowers, no matter how numerous they may be.

The 20 walks in this book are all circular and range in length from $2^1/_4$ to $6^3/_4$ miles and all but one start at or close to a public house where refreshments may be obtained. For the walks that start at a pub the publicans have consented to patrons leaving their cars in the pub car park while they walk (please ask first) and in all cases I have suggested alternative parking close by. I have also given information about nearby attractions so that you may make a whole day of it if you wish.

Most of the routes are pretty level but one or two do contain a hill or two and I have made mention of this in the individual walk introduction. For your convenience the text is divided into numbered paragraphs that correspond to numbers on my sketch maps, and should you wish to follow the routes in more detail I recommend you take along an Ordnance Survey map that will give you added detail of the area. Sheet numbers 176, 186 and 187 of the Landranger series cover all the walks in this book and are a small and worthwhile investment.

If travelling by public transport it is best to contact the bus or train operator first as timetables may vary. For buses contact the Surrey Travel Line on 01737 223000 and for trains contact the National Train Information Service on 0345 484950.

For footwear I would recommend stout walking shoes or boots as these offer support on uneven or slippery ground. Binoculars and a good field guide will be invaluable aids in helping you spot and identify the wildlife you will see on these rambles.

Finally, I hope that you enjoy these walks of discovery in this varied and ever-interesting county.

David Weller

THORPE GREEN, CALLOW HILL AND STROUDE

– *field paths and indigenous woodland*

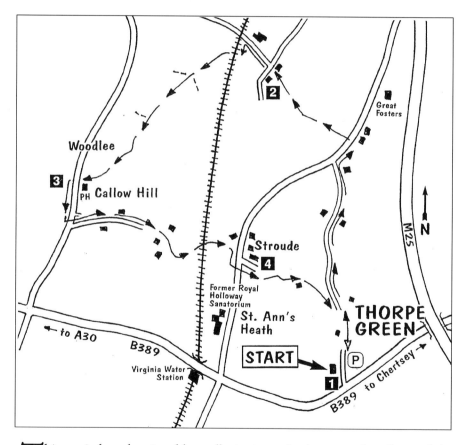

*T*his varied and enjoyable walk starts at the large and well cared for open space of Thorpe Green, an ideal picnic spot. The route passes along field paths and through meadows where the quiet rambler may see grey herons preening themselves and the occasional roe deer grazing. The route then gradually climbs Callow Hill through peaceful indigenous mixed woodland.

The descent from Callow Hill through more woodland takes the rambler past attractive houses in part of the rather exclusive Virginia Water domain. Soon our way continues through the small hamlet of Stroude – built to serve the needs of the former Royal Holloway Sanatorium – before we meet up again with the expanse of Thorpe Green.

THE WALK

1 Walk away from the B389 and cross the large green and keep roughly parallel to a small lane on your left to reach tennis courts. Pass to the left of these and go under the boughs of a well proportioned oak to reach a broad path on your left in 30 yards. Soon this path reaches a quiet lane where you continue ahead for 2/3 of a mile to reach a T-junction. Turn rightwards here and press on alongside the road towards a couple of white cottages. Before these are reached, turn left on a footpath signposted to Callow Hill. After a while this narrow path, bordered by tall foxgloves during summer, crosses a stream and ends by a field where

STARTING POINT: At the car park on Thorpe Green opposite the Rose and Crown. This attractive pub, set back from the road, is open from 11 am to 3 pm and 5.30 pm to 11 pm each day (10.30 pm Sunday) and all day on Saturdays. The pub serves good pub food at lunchtimes and evenings throughout the week and at lunchtimes only on weekends. There is a large

garden for your further enjoyment on a warm summer's day. Telephone: 01344 845154.

HOW TO GET THERE: Thorpe Green is on the B389, 2 miles west of the centre of Chertsey. From Chertsey take the B388 towards Thorpe and at a roundabout by the M25 overpass go left on the B389 under the M25 to soon reach Thorpe Green and the car park by the Rose and Crown pub.
    London United Busways serve the area.

PARKING: Parking is free in the car park on Thorpe Green.

LENGTH OF WALK: 4½ miles. Map: OS Landranger 176 West London area (GR 012680).

you cross a stile. Bear right here and continue along the right-hand field edge. If you are quiet you may get the chance to observe a grey heron preening itself in this sometimes waterlogged field. Ahead above the trees you will see the towers of the splendid Victorian buildings of the Royal Holloway and Bedford New College at Englefield Green. Cross a stile between two cottages and go out to a small lane.

2 Turn right for a few yards and then left to continue along a road named Prune Hill for a short while. Turn left in front of an unmanned level crossing on a footpath signposted to Callow Hill. Within

yards and with caution, cross the railway track and press on along a line of trees on the right edge of a meadow. The last time I came this way I spotted a roe deer *(see Walk 15)* quietly grazing among the tall grasses that include torgrass, cock's-foot and meadow fescue. Cross a gravel driveway to meet a wooden fingerboard. Keep ahead and pass to the left of this signpost and after 30 yards or so cross a stile and enter peaceful mixed woodland where squirrels and woodland birds abound. Bear left on an uphill path where you pass under wild cherry trees. Stay on the well trodden path through this lovely mixed woodland and ignore any side paths. In the more open sunlit areas during summer you may well see purple hairstreak butterflies. Their eggs are laid on oak twigs close to leaf buds and hatch after about nine months. Eventually the path broadens and ends at a road alongside the Rose & Olive Branch, a conveniently placed public house owned by the Morland Brewery.

3 Go leftwards on the footpath of this uphill road. After passing a bend, turn left into a quiet road named Hollow Lane and pass a rather

The foxglove, also known as fairy gloves, is a highly poisonous plant that for centuries has been invaluable for its medical uses. The alkaloid digitalis which is extracted from the leaves helps regulate the action of the heart and stimulates the kidneys to excrete the excess water retained by people with heart problems. In its fresh state it is highly dangerous especially to children and livestock and can cause drowsiness, convulsions and in some cases, death.

The common water plantain, growing from 30 cm to 100 cm in height, is found along the muddy edges of slow moving brooks and streams. The tall, graceful stem bears a cluster of pale pink flowers which only open in the afternoon during summer months. These are followed by distinctive flattened seeds arranged in a horizontal whorl. For centuries the rhizome and leaves have been collected and used as a treatment for cystitis, kidney stones and dysentery.

exclusive nursing home. When the road ends continue ahead between posts on a broad track. Later cross a tarmac drive and proceed ahead on a downhill path that takes you through woodland and down a deep gully to reach the railway track once again. As the sign says, stop, look and listen before you cross. Maintain direction past farm buildings and a house to reach a road in the hamlet of Stroude. Turn rightwards along this road and then soon turn left into a cul-de-sac named The Lane.

4 At the end of this short road continue to the left on a bridleway that skirts a field. Cross a small bridge over a slow moving stream where the graceful water plantain grows and press on along a made-up path. After passing a few houses set well back from the lane, a T-junction is met. Turn rightwards here and soon the tennis courts at Thorpe Green are reached where another rightwards turn takes you over the green to the car park and the end of the walk.

PLACE OF INTEREST NEARBY
Savill Garden, just one mile west of Englefield Green, is a 35 acre woodland garden where water is a feature. Laid out in 1932 by the then deputy ranger of Windsor Great Park, Eric Savill, this wonderful garden forms the south-eastern boundary to the park itself. The garden is a spectacular sight during early summer when the banks of rhododendrons break into colour. There is also a plant shop and restaurant. Open all year round from 10 am to 6 pm, or sunset if earlier. Telephone: 01784 435544.

WALK 2

CHOBHAM COMMON AND ALBURY BOTTOM
– *rare heathland habitats*

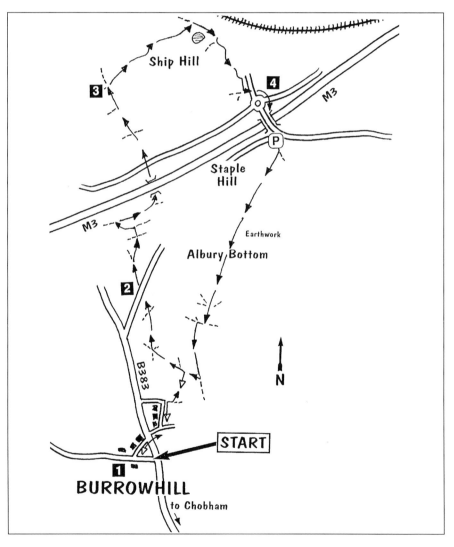

*T*his is an easy walk across the sandy soil of Chobham Common, a National Nature Reserve and the largest area of heathland remaining in south-east England. Fine views are gained from vantage points on the sandy ridges that the route passes and very little sign of human activity can be seen from them.

Cattle ceased grazing on Chobham Common some 80 years or so ago and since then silver birch has started to invade the heath and upset the delicate ecological balance of this rapidly disappearing heathland habitat. Also helping to maintain the balance here was the rabbit but unfortunately the 1950s' myxomatosis epidemic all but wiped out the population. Even though rabbit numbers are recovering, Surrey County Council periodically clears the young trees to preserve this habitat. The council also uses a herd of cattle to graze on the purple moor grass that grows so aggressively and suppresses the other plants. Chobham Common supports many rare species of ants, wasps and spiders as well as the rare smooth snake.

STARTING POINT: In Windlesham Road, Burrowhill alongside a small triangular green complete with village pump and forge. It makes the ideal spot to start a ramble and you can stock up for a picnic along the route with scrumptious filled rolls and cold drinks from the Burrowhill Bakery that overlooks the green. You may of course prefer your

refreshments before or after the walk in the Four Horseshoes public house opposite where traditional pub food and ales are served. Telephone: 01276 857581.

HOW TO GET THERE: Burrowhill is a small rural community ½ mile north of Chobham. From Chobham village head north along Windsor Road (B383) and the second road to your left will be Windlesham Road.

Tillingbourne Buses and North Surrey Buses serve the area.

PARKING: In Windlesham Road and around the green.

LENGTH OF WALK: 4³/₄ miles. Map: OS Landranger 176 West London area (GR 970628).

THE WALK

1 Walk across the green towards the Four Horseshoes and then cross the B383 to continue along Gorse Lane opposite. Within yards bear left into a quiet rural lane named Heather Way. When this lane bends sharply leftwards go right on a broad track and within yards bear leftwards and continue along a pleasant bridleway. Soon, with a five bar gate ahead of you by a crossing track, turn left. At a junction of paths a few yards before passing under power cables, bear right at a fork and continue on the main bridleway. Soon go over a crossing track and maintain direction ahead to reach a road. Whilst walking this way one bright October morning I was delighted to see dozens of the brightly coloured fly agaric fungi along the route.

2 Cross the road diagonally rightwards and continue along a bridleway that passes under chestnut trees where during the autumn pocketfuls of fresh chestnuts lie in abundance on the ground. When the path leaves the trees and crosses open heath bear right at a fork and continue along the wider track. Ignore a crossing track and maintain direction up a shingle slope. From the top of this ridge it is possible to see some of the vast area that Chobham Common covers. Imagine how remote and peaceful it would be without the inglorious M3 motorway marring the quietness of the area. During early summer there is a blaze of yellow from the gorse that grows and flowers here in profusion. Gorse, or furze as it is also called, is a member of the pea family and can in fact flower at any time of the year, giving rise to the old saying that 'kissing's out of season

Tufted vetch, a member of the pea family, seen here climbing over brambles was once a valuable fodder plant. The pea-like violet-blue flowers are followed by brown pods that each contain up to six seeds. There are numerous nodules on the branching roots which contain nitrogen-fixing bacteria that are capable of transforming nitrogen from the air into nitrogenous compounds that enrich the soil.

Fly agaric – the toadstool of the pixies – is bright red with white spots. This toadstool is highly poisonous and contains the hallucinogenic toxin muscarine as do several other common poisonous toadstools. Although it has been estimated that about 250 grams would need to be ingested for a fatal dose in the case of a healthy adult a child would need far less. Don't let any small teeth marks you may see fool you into believing it is edible – it is not! Some small mammals are immune to its poison. In the past it has been used in many religions where after drying in the sun one was taken to produce a trance-like state – not to be recommended.

when the gorse is out of bloom'. If you are walking this way on a hot summer's day you may wonder what the continuous cracking noise is that seems to follow you wherever you go. Well, it's the seed pods of the gorse popping in the sun and throwing their seeds several feet. Later, ants disperse the seeds even further. At a T-junction on top of this ridge you should turn left. After descending from the ridge a second T-junction is met where the way is to the right along a path that remains parallel to the motorway. Later bear left at a fork and within yards pass under the motorway and press on ahead, leaving the noise of the traffic behind you. Soon cross a road and maintain direction along the gravelly path ahead where during summer tufted vetch climbs over the scrub.

3 The path eventually goes up an incline where you pass a welcoming seat and 30 yards later the crest of the hill is reached by a junction of tracks. Turn right here and continue along a narrower pretty path that offers lovely views over the common and where you are likely to see a kestrel hovering in search of prey. The kestrel is easily identified as it has perfected its hover so well that no other hawk can match it. From high up it will search for any movement that indicates the presence of a mouse, vole or even a beetle. Having sighted its prey it will dive at alarming speed and grab the prey with its powerful talons. Like the sparrowhawk *(see Walk 12)* it then flies off with its kill to a favourite 'plucking post'. At a T-junction turn right and continue along the main

15

track where a heathland pool hidden away on your right is passed. This is the territory of the dragonfly, another efficient hunter *(see Walk 18)*. Ignore smaller paths to left and right and keep to the wide track. Continue along the track when it turns sharply right by a barrier alongside a road. Soon after this by a junction of paths, turn left and pass a barrier to reach a quiet lane. Turn right here and continue along the lane to reach a roundabout.

4 With caution, as there are no footpaths, pass the roundabout and cross the bridge over the motorway. Ignore a road immediately to your right and press on ahead to reach a small parking area in Staple Hill Road. Pass through the parking area and press on ahead along the broad track and soon bear rightwards at a fork. Continue along this lovely track as it passes through the wild scenery of Albury Bottom. Silver birch is one of our indigenous trees and was the first tree to colonise Britain after the Ice Age. To stop it getting too much of a foothold on Albury Bottom and upsetting the delicate balance of the heathland, Surrey County Council periodically poison the young trees. It is also along this gentle valley that a herd of cattle are sometimes employed to graze on the invasive purple moor grass, again to maintain the balance of the area. Eventually a junction of paths by pine trees is met where you should maintain direction ahead to soon meet a T-junction and go rightwards. In 30 yards by another junction of paths turn left and soon pass under power cables. When a footpath is met to your right you should take this and pass between two fields. At the end of the field to your left, turn left along the broad bridleway walked earlier to reach Heather Way and Gorse Lane and soon Windlesham Road and the end of the ramble.

PLACE OF INTEREST NEARBY
Brooklands Museum, the birthplace of British motor racing. Allow yourself plenty of time for this interesting trip down motor racing's memory lane. A section of the famous racing circuit still exists where the terrifying banking rises 30 feet above your head. As well as displays of classic racing cars there are historic buildings and aircraft that reinforce the fact that Brooklands was also an airfield. Open every Saturday, Sunday and bank holiday from 10 am to 5 pm during April to September and 10 am to 4 pm between October and January. The museum can be found on the B374, 1½ miles south of Weybridge. Telephone: 01932 857381.

PIRBRIGHT, FOX CORNER AND STANFORD BROOK

– alder, birch and babbling brooks

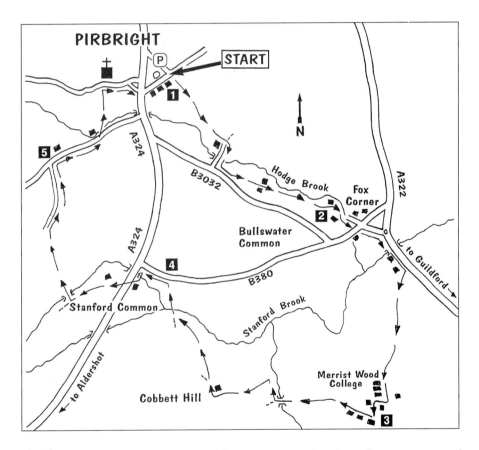

*T*his mainly woodland ramble starts at Pirbright village green and follows the route of a small stream where we pass the remains of Heath Mill, a watermill that now makes a handsome residence. The route meets Stanford Brook at Fox Corner alongside an area set aside for wildlife before returning through the grounds of Merrist Wood College – a seat of learning for wildlife and countryside conservation.

Later the route passes over Stanford Common where the scenery changes to heathland with birch and heather. A good range of wildlife and plants can always be seen on this ramble as the route passes through a variety of habitats that include mature oak woodland and heathland bog. This is a wonderfully varied walk for any time of the year although it has to be said that in winter after prolonged rain a couple of small sections along the route can become waterlogged, but nothing a good pair of wellingtons couldn't cope with.

THE WALK

1 Take the public footpath that runs along the driveway to the left of the Cricketers and soon pass a gate to continue through a plant nursery. Follow the waymarked sign rightwards as it directs you past greenhouses. At the end of a pine planting area press on ahead through mixed woodland where, during winter, you will see plenty of fungi. The path soon leads you over a small brook and a stile where you enter a field and continue diagonally rightwards to another stile. Cross this to

STARTING POINT: At the Cricketers Inn public house opposite Pirbright village green and pond. This popular pub owned by Allied Domecq boasts an outside children's play area and a pleasant secluded garden for sunny summer days. It is necessary to book if wishing to eat here on Sundays. Telephone: 01483 473198.

HOW TO GET THERE: Pirbright is 4^1/$_2$ miles north of the A3 at Guildford and sits astride the A324. When entering the village from the south turn immediately right at the village green. The Cricketers pub is on the right opposite the pond.

Tillingbourne Buses and Arriva Buses serve the village.

PARKING: Patrons of the Cricketers may use the pub car park while they walk (please ask first). There is also free parking alongside the pond or further around the green.

LENGTH OF WALK: 5^3/$_4$ miles. Map: OS Landranger 186 Aldershot, Guildford and surrounding area (GR 947559).

soon reach a driveway alongside the lovely old house at Whites Farm. Turn right along this drive and soon after crossing the Hodge Brook a road is met where you now turn left. In 120 yards bear left on a path lined by dozens of holly trees where there was not a berry to be seen the last time I came along here in winter. It could be that it is too shaded along this path for the trees to flower. At a tarmac drive by a couple of houses keep ahead and very soon at a T-junction maintain direction ahead on a path leading through peaceful oak and birch woodland. The path shadows the course of the Hodge Brook which is through the trees to your left. The easily identified fly agaric fungi (*see Walk 2*) can be seen in these woods during late summer and autumn. At the end of this pretty piece of woodland continue leftwards along a driveway.

2 Immediately after crossing the Hodge Brook you pass Heath Mill with its derelict overshot waterwheel. The mill building itself now makes a pretty private residence but its industrial past is easy to spot. Press on along this drive and pass more houses to finally meet a main road alongside the Fox public house. Maintain direction ahead along the road to reach a small roundabout by an area given over to wildlife. As well as the Stanford Brook there is a coppice and a wild flower meadow where sparrowhawks and owls hunt. Amongst the butterflies that are encouraged to breed here are the small skipper, red admiral, speckled wood, painted lady, brimstone and

The alder, pictured in February, is seen here displaying the previous year's spent female seed cones together with the new year's male catkins. The tree is adapted for growing in wet marshy areas where, with sedges, it will eventually take over and form a wet woodland habitat called alder carr. Alder was heavily coppiced for its light, durable wood used in turnery and at one time clog making. Charcoal from alder was used in making black gunpowder while the bark was used in the tanning process. When newly cut the bright orange wood was also a source of dye.

holly blue to name just a few. Turn right here along the A322 and soon cross Stanford Brook and pass the Old Mill House. Opposite you will see the distinctive building of Rickford Mill and by the entrance gate is one of its grindstones. Continue along the road and 70 yards or so after passing a bakery turn right and cross a field. Follow the waymarked signs over fields owned by Merrist Wood College, where you cross a good variety of stiles. After passing a willow coppice you continue alongside greenhouses to finally pass through a squeeze stile alongside a gate and meet a junction of small roads.

3 Turn right here and then left as the signs direct you between classrooms to meet a road. Turn rightwards along this road and again pass classrooms and later a tennis court. At a visitor parking bay by the reception building continue ahead over an open piece of mown grass, keeping to the right-hand edge. The path now passes between a wire fence and the edge of oak woodland where at the foot of a slope you cross two stiles in quick succession to meet a farm track. Press on and go over another stile ahead of you by a gate. Ignore a stile on your right in 60 yards and turn right immediately after crossing a small stream. The dominant tree in this damp woodland is the alder, a water-loving tree, and you will see many fine specimens along the edge of the stream. At the end of a wire fence by a post turn left and skirt a golf course. Keep parallel to the golf course and you will eventually reach a drive by the gateway of a large house. Cross the drive and continue along a path that skirts the garden. Ignore a left fork and remain on the main path as it first goes through woodland and then narrows as it leads you over heathland and passes a clear peat pool where during summer dragonflies (*see Walk 18*) hover over the sphagnum moss in search of prey. Eventually this narrow path meets a larger track where you should now bear right and re-cross the Stanford Brook to reach a road.

4 Turn left along the road and at a T-junction turn left again. A few yards after passing the Royal Oak pub turn right on a bridleway that goes through pine and birch woodland. You will see a few birch trees with bracket fungus growing on them. Unlike most fungi these are parasites that live on healthy wood, healthy that is until the fungi causes the tree to decay and die. After about $1/4$ mile turn right on a signposted footpath and soon cross a stile and press on through damp mature woodland. Cross a small stream and maintain direction on this path until it eventually meets a broad farm track where you again maintain direction. When this track meets an unmade lane bear rightwards along the lane. There is a large and rather dilapidated Scots pine along here with a succession of woodpecker holes in the boughs.

5 At a T-junction turn right and press on along this quiet and pleasant road passing a welcome seat. Soon you will pass the pretty mill pond at Manor Farm where the typical mill buildings built into the bank are now a private residence. Soon after crossing the mill stream bear left on a footpath by the gateway to The Manor House. Maintain direction along this pretty path as it crosses two fields to reach a lane. The meadow pipit frequents these fields and this little bird has the dubious distinction of being the most likely host to a cuckoo's egg which it devotedly strives to rear as its own. No mean feat when the young hatchling is at least twice its own size. Turn right along the lane which passes St Michael's church and graveyard where you will see the huge granite obelisk marking the grave of Sir Henry Morton Stanley, the writer and explorer who travelled through darkest Africa to find Dr Livingstone. The wall alongside the road here has the pretty ivy-leaved toadflax plant growing on it. A little further along this lane you will arrive back at Pirbright village green, the Cricketers Inn and the end of the walk.

PLACE OF INTEREST NEARBY
Boat trips along the Basingstoke Canal are available on the *Painted Lady*, a traditional narrow boat that carries 12 passengers. Trips are available from the end of March to the end of September on Wednesdays and Sundays plus bank and school holidays from 11 am to 4 pm. The boat is located at Monument Bridge, Monument Road, Woking. Telephone: 01483 725527.

WALK 4

SHEEPLEAS AND MOUNTAIN WOOD

– *a woodland wonderland*

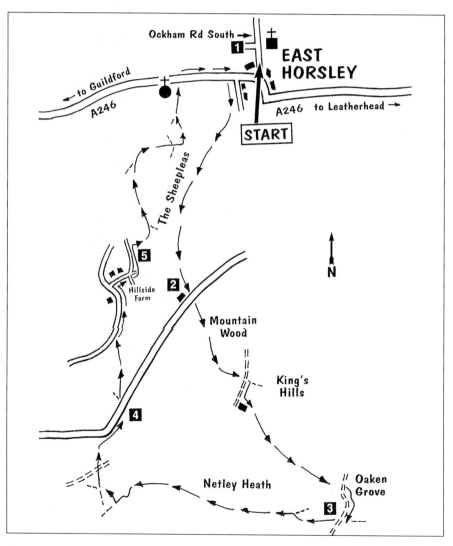

*T*his is a wonderfully picturesque walk through a part of the Surrey
Hills which is designated as an Area of Outstanding Natural Beauty.
The route through woodland covering the northern slopes of the North
Downs passes a variety of habitats including hazel coppice, mature oak
and beech, and wild flower-filled meadows and clearings.

Large areas of this woodland were opened up by the hurricane of 1987 and
these have been colonised by the many wild flowers that now grow here.
The area offers cover to many butterflies, birds – the green woodpecker
being a common sight here – and larger mammals such as badgers and
roe deer. The ramble contains one steepish ascent and descent.

THE WALK

1 From Ockham Road South walk back to the A246 and turn right
where you pass the Duke of Wellington pub. Continue alongside
the road and 100 yards after passing Longhurst Road go left on a broad
public bridleway and pass a Sheepleas information sign. After skirting a
small hazel coppice the track continues through a ribbon of mature trees.
As you enter woodland you will see on your left the charcoal ovens that

STARTING POINT: Alongside St
Martin's church in Ockham
Road South. The route soon
passes the Duke of Wellington
public house. Ample bar
snacks are available here and
the pub also boasts a good
restaurant area and full menu.
Telephone: 01483 282164.

HOW TO GET THERE: From
Leatherhead take the A246
towards Guildford.
Immediately after passing

Horsley Towers on the second part of a tight S-bend turn right into Ockham
Road South. From Guildford take the A246 towards Leatherhead and on the
first part of the S-bend by Horsley Towers turn left into Ockham Road South.
    Arriva Buses and London & County Buses serve the area.

PARKING: Along the roadside in Ockham Road South near St Martin's church.

LENGTH OF WALK: 6½ miles. Map: OS Landranger 187 Dorking, Reigate
and Crawley area (GR 095526).

produce good quality eco-friendly charcoal. Soon, at a junction of tracks by a post keep ahead. Soon at another junction of tracks keep ahead on the main track signposted to Green Dene car park. Maintain direction at all times and ignore paths on either side. I have seen a great variety of birds along this track including green woodpeckers, jays, carrion crows, coal, blue and great tits plus one or two pheasants. Pheasants have the nasty habit of remaining still and unseen until you are almost on them, and then with a great flurry of wings and undergrowth they fly off, leaving you to calm yourself before continuing along the way. Eventually the track descends to a small road by a house.

2 Cross the road and continue ahead on a stony uphill path with moss covered banks. Soon the path starts to descend into the next valley. The dominant tree here becomes the pine, planted as a crop for its quick and straight growth. Watch your step here if the path is muddy as the descent is rather steep. At the valley bottom a logging track is met where you now turn right and pass a gate. Stacked up on either side of the track are piles of logs from oak, beech, chestnut and pine trees. This woodland is actively managed and while on this short track please be aware that heavy logging equipment also uses it. When the logging camp and sawmill are reached, bear left on a bridleway that passes to the rear of the

Charcoal burning is carried out in the woodland around Sheepleas. The timber, usually ash or hornbeam, is cut into 60 cm lengths and placed vertically on a platform of thinner logs that provide an updraught for the main charge. Any gaps are filled with smaller logs and with the lid propped open the oven is lit through vents around the base. After an hour most of the lower vents are sealed and the lid is firmly put in place, leaving a couple of chimneys. After 24 hours when the smoke turns yellow, the remaining vents and chimneys are sealed to exclude all air; 24 hours after that the oven is opened and the resulting charcoal, now weighing only two-thirds of its original weight, is ready for bagging-up and selling. If you wish to use local charcoal from sites such as this it is available from most B&Q stores. For more information contact the Bioregional Development Group on 020 8773 2322.

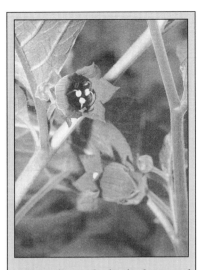

*D*eadly nightshade (pictured flowering in July) grows up to 1.5 m tall and is found in the woods around Sheepleas. This quite rare plant is often confused with the much more common bittersweet or woody nightshade. The purplish bell-shaped flowers are followed by black, very poisonous cherry-like berries – three or four being enough to kill a child. The name nightshade is derived from an Anglo-Saxon word for narcotic. Despite being highly poisonous the plant has been used for centuries in medicine and cosmetics. The latter for blanching the skin and removing freckles of actresses in the last century, hence its common name belladonna (fair lady).

buildings. The rising track now follows a valley bottom through an area known as the King's Hills. Press on along this lovely track with glorious patches of foxgloves in summer and ferns during autumn. Ignore paths to left and right until finally, after passing holly trees, a T-junction is met. Turn right here along the wide track and in 50 yards follow it round to the left. The habitat now changes to a more natural one of oak and ferns and soon you find yourself on top of the North Downs with panoramic views ahead of you.

3 Continue ahead with glimpses over the weald to the South Downs until a North Downs Way signpost is reached. Turn right and follow the waymarked long distance path. By a Hackhurst Downs sign and seat turn left along the waymarked broad level track which is partially metalled. We are now back among our native trees that during autumn display their golden colours in the sunlight. I have walked this way in autumn during a cold snap and witnessed clouds of leaves falling in unison as the sun melts the frost. At a seat engraved 'Gravel Hill Gate' keep ahead. This seat marks the halfway point to the ramble. Soon after passing an S-bend in the track turn right by a post along another track and pass a second post. When a track on the right joins our way keep left and soon, at an angled crossing path, turn right and continue on this stony path that soon meets yet another forestry track. Cross this and maintain direction ahead on a path bordered by larch trees. The larch is a deciduous pine and in the early 18th century it was only grown for its splendour. In more recent times its wood has been much valued in the use of telegraph poles and fencing. Apparently it was also used for pit props as it never gave way without first issuing a loud warning crack. Continue along this very pleasant track until a small road is reached.

4 Maintain direction along the road and in 150 yards bear left on a path that has a wire fence to the left and a dense pine plantation on the right. This type of plantation offers nothing to wildlife as the trees are so densely packed that no light reaches the forest floor. This together with a deep layer of pine needles will stop any other plant life from growing. Birds avoid these areas as few insects will be found to feed on. To your left in the more open and natural woodland strip I have seen roe deer peacefully grazing (*see Walk 15*). In a short while the fenced path continues between fields where occasionally pheasants feed along the field edges. What makes some people shoot these magnificent birds for fun is beyond me. Before long a small road is reached where you should turn right. At the top of a steepish incline turn right at a signposted bridleway along a concrete driveway. Pass between farm buildings and at a junction of driveways turn left.

5 At the end of the field to your right, turn right on a narrow path lined with the humble field maple, so often relegated to hedgerows. During autumn their brilliant leaf colours contrast well with the gaudy seed pods of the spindle tree that also grows here. Soon the path takes you away from the field edge and you meet a T-junction. Bear leftwards here and keep ahead on this track, ignoring all others. When a larger track sweeps in from the left bear rightwards along it. The track soon runs parallel to a field at the end of which is a junction of paths by a post. Maintain direction ahead up a small grassy incline to reach a seat by a cowslip meadow. Turn left here and soon pass along the left edge of a second meadow. Go through a gate and bear rightwards along a broad farm track that eventually brings you to the A246 alongside St Mary's church. Turn right here to soon reach the Duke of Wellington pub and the end of the walk.

PLACE OF INTEREST NEARBY

Hatchlands House was built for Admiral Boscawen in the 1750s and is set in beautiful parkland. Within the house are interiors by Robert Adam and the Cobbe Collection, the world's largest collection of keyboard instruments. Open from the beginning of April to the end of October on Tuesdays, Wednesdays, Thursdays and Sundays from 2 pm to 5.30 pm, Hatchlands is 1$^1/_2$ miles west of East Horsley off the A246. Telephone: 01483 222482.

EFFINGHAM AND GREAT BOOKHAM COMMONS

– *oak, blackthorn and enchanting ponds*

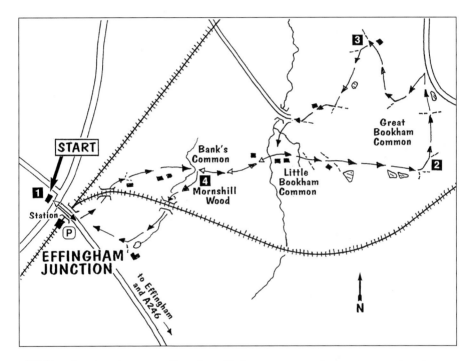

*T*his fascinating woodland walk is across ancient commonland once owned by Lord Howard of Effingham. Lord Howard was Lord High Admiral of the British Navy and it was under his command that Sir Francis Drake defeated the Spanish Armada in 1588. Now owned by the National Trust, these 452 acres of commonland lie in an area where London clay meets the chalk of the North Downs. Small streams wind their way through the oak woodland to form ponds and marshy areas that in turn create a habitat where many diverse plants and animals live.

Countless birds and plants associated with both woodland and water will be seen along the pretty route and the quiet rambler may by lucky and spot a roe deer or two. Because of the clay soil in the woodland some paths can become quite muddy, but not impassable, during winter or after prolonged rain.

THE WALK

1 With your back to the Lord Howard pub, cross Forest Road and continue along Howard Road where you soon pass Effingham Junction Station and the pay and display car park. Just 20 yards after passing a bus stop turn left on a permissive path along a wide track through woodland owned by the Woodland Trust. Pass under a railway bridge and at a junction of tracks ignore the side tracks and press on ahead on a public bridleway. Continue along the main path as it crosses Bank's Common. Wood pigeons are a common sight around here and when disturbed fly off with a great clatter of wings. Much shyer and more

STARTING POINT: At the Lord Howard public house in Forest Road, Effingham Junction. A wide selection of food is on offer which includes children's, vegetarian and pizza selections. A large garden, patio and children's area are available for you to relax in on summer days. It is not necessary to book unless you are in a sizeable party. Telephone: 01483 282572 or 01483 281516.

HOW TO GET THERE: Effingham Junction is found 2 miles north of Effingham. From the A246 Guildford Road in Effingham turn into The Street and after 2 miles you pass Effingham Junction Station. The Lord Howard is 200 yards further on at a road junction with Forest Road.

Arriva Buses, North Surrey Buses and South West Trains serve the area

PARKING: Patrons of the Lord Howard may, with prior permission, use the pub car park while they walk. There is alternative parking in a large pay and display car park alongside the station. This car park is free on bank holidays and weekends and only a small charge is made after 10 am on weekdays.

LENGTH OF WALK: 5^1/$_2$ miles. Map: OS Landranger 187 Dorking, Reigate and Crawley area (GR 103560).

wary than the feral pigeons that frequent our towns, they live mainly on grain, peas and beans and if in a large flock will do great damage to crops. Soon after passing a couple of houses and crossing a small stream you should turn leftwards at a fork and continue along a path that crosses Bookham Common. Stay on the main path and maintain direction and pass a small parking area. Again continue ahead on the broad track and soon, through trees on your right, you will notice a series of ponds. Carry on along the track a little further to meet a large junction of tracks.

2 Bear left at a fork in the track at this junction and in 80 yards bear leftwards again at a second fork and pass between posts. The route now continues on a slightly rising and narrower woodland path. Roe deer (*see Walk 15*) seem to like grazing alongside this path so on a quiet day you may get a glimpse. At a second set of posts press on ahead to the crest of the slope and go over a crossing track to maintain direction. After passing a small car parking area, the path continues parallel to a road and passes a small woodland pool. Some 200 yards after this pool and before the path reaches the road, turn sharply left on a narrower path signposted 'NT'. At a fork in this path bear rightwards on a path that remains parallel to a field edge. Cross a stile and go forward on a path that runs along a ribbon of trees. It may be possible to spot the purple hairstreak and speckled wood butterflies here.

*B*lackthorn can form dense thickets as you will see on parts of this walk. The shrub has vicious thorns at the tip of each branch which are so strong that they are capable of piercing a horse or cow's hoof, sometimes causing severe blood poisoning. The shrub has an early flowering season which gives rise to the term 'blackthorn winter' as the weather can still be bitterly cold during March, its flowering time. The fruit of the blackthorn is the sloe, a small, bitter, plum-like fruit that is used to flavour sloe gin. In Ireland the polished wood is used to make the short shillelaghs that are still sold to tourists.

3 After passing to the rear of a house two stiles are met. Ignore the stile ahead and turn left over a stile in the corner of a field and continue on a path along the field edge, signposted to Bookham Common. An easily spotted bird along here is the yellowhammer, especially the male with its bright lemon coloured head and underside. In 100 yards at the end of woodland go diagonally half left to cross the field to a further stile. Re-enter woodland where you soon pass another woodland pool. Keep ahead along this path and soon after going through posts turn right on a crossing track. Some time after passing the rear of farm buildings a T-junction is reached where you should turn right. Very soon a small lane and a bridge over a stream is reached. The route now follows a small path on the left immediately before the bridge. Go through posts and cross a wooden bridge and soon pass a thicket of blackthorn where in spring the bushes flower en masse and during autumn an array of their plum-like fruit will be seen. Press on ahead to meet a broad crossing track by a house. Turn right here and retrace your earlier steps along this level track.

4 Soon after a field on your right ends by a National Trust sign you should turn left on a narrow path through pretty woodland. During spring the banks of the small stream here are lined by groups of primroses. Cross a wooden bridge and stile and press on ahead alongside a hedgerow. Cross a stile and go under a railway bridge to a second stile which you also cross. Press on ahead alongside a ditch and cross the field to another stile. Cross this and pass the garden and ornamental pond of a large house. At the end of the garden cross another stile. Bear half right here and press on along a path through trees that eventually brings you to the permissive path walked earlier. Turn left to meet the road and turn right along it to reach the Lord Howard pub and the end of the walk.

PLACE OF INTEREST NEARBY
Clandon Park, a Palladian mansion 250 years old, is notable for its magnificent Marble Hall. The house contains a superb collection of 18th century furniture, porcelain, textiles and carpets. The gardens contain, amongst other things, a Maori house and sunken Dutch garden. Clandon Park is 3 miles east of Guildford off the A247 at West Clandon. Telephone: 01483 222482.

FARTHING DOWNS
AND HAPPY VALLEY

– rolling chalk downland

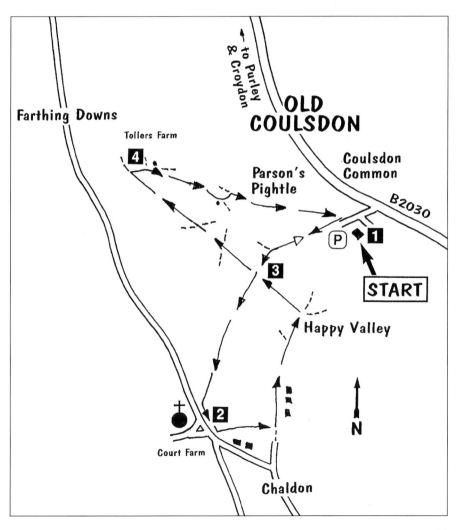

*T*his enthralling walk is a real treat for the wild flower lover for both the short and longer versions cross a flower-filled valley to reach the fine old Norman church of St Peter and St Paul at Chaldon. After passing through woodland the route returns to the valley floor where during early summer, wild flowers will be seen en masse – yellow rattle, meadow cranesbill and fairy flax to name but a few – so take a field guide with you to see how many you can identify.

The longer walk continues through this Arcadian scenery before returning along higher ground where I spotted three species of orchid displaying themselves quite admirably among the chalkland grasses. Both routes contain one steepish ascent and descent.

THE WALK

1 With your back to the B2030 continue along Fox Lane to a large parking area. Pass a gate and continue ahead on a tarmac path with a meadow on your left. At the end of this path press on ahead down a stony path between trees. Just 20 yards after rounding a right-hand bend turn left

STARTING POINT: At the Fox public house in Fox Lane, Old Coulsdon where there is a good sized garden and patio area that can be used during fine weather. Telephone: 01583 330401.

HOW TO GET THERE: Old Coulsdon is 6 miles south of the centre of Croydon. From the A23 Brighton Road turn south-east into Stoats Nest Road (B2030), 1 mile south of Purley. When the open area of Coulsdon Common is reached turn right by a bus stop into Fox Lane. The Fox will soon be seen to your left.

Epsom Buses and International Coach Lines serve the area.

PARKING: Patrons of the Fox may use its car park, with prior permission, while they walk. There is also a large parking area a few yards further along Fox Lane.

LENGTH OF WALK: 2¹/₄ or 4 miles. Map: OS Landranger 187 Dorking, Reigate and Crawley area (GR 317568).

on a narrow downhill path signposted to Ditches Lane. Cross a path in the valley below and continue up the incline ahead. At the top maintain direction through a band of woodland to reach a field. Cross this field and the next, keeping to the well trodden path to avoid damaging any crops. At the end of the second field a lane is reached where you turn left.

2 Continue along the lane for a short distance and pass the ancient church of St Peter and St Paul that lies hidden by the trees to your right. Soon turn left on a path signposted to Piles Wood. At a T-junction with an unmade driveway turn left along the drive and when this abruptly ends press on ahead along a narrower path. The way is now through peaceful mixed woodland where on warm summer days the scent of honeysuckle hangs in the air. Ignore a stile to your left as the path gradually descends to the valley floor where a junction of paths is met. Turn leftwards at this junction and stroll through this peaceful scene with wild flowers carpeting the valley sides. There is a good array of grassland flowers to be seen here during spring and early summer including patches of meadow cranesbill. Part of the geranium family, this pretty plant has a much bluer flower than other cranesbills. Pass through a wide gap in a hawthorn hedge ahead.

3 *Those wishing to only complete the shorter ramble should turn right immediately after passing through the hawthorn hedge. Retrace your steps uphill to reach the tarmac path that leads you back to the Fox public house.* For the longer route keep ahead along the valley floor. If anything, the number of wild flower species increases here and the semi-parasite yellow rattle

Yellow rattle, also known as cock's-comb, is unusual in that it is partially parasitic. The roots of the plant attach themselves to its host and through them it withdraws nutrients and water. Yellow rattle is very variable in size and grows from about 7 cm to 60 cm in height. Here they are quite short and don't pop their heads up much above the height of the grasses. The common name yellow rattle is derived from the bladder-like seed capsules which, when mature, rattle in the wind.

The pyramidal orchid pictured here is fairly common on chalk downland in the south of England. It is easily spotted amongst the other orchids that grow here because of its squat, pyramidal shaped flower spike. Pollinated by butterflies and moths the flower spike ranges in colour from pale to dark pink and has a strong and rather unpleasant smell.

grows en masse. Green woodpeckers may be seen feeding on the ant hills in these meadows. Ignore paths to left and right and continue forward until the path goes into a band of woodland.

4 Turn right along the edge of this woodland to very soon cross a bridlepath. The route now continues diagonally rightwards uphill across the face of the valley side on a narrow chalky path. This is one of the best places to spot orchids in Surrey. It was along this slope one fine June day that I saw three different species of orchid including the pyramidal orchid, flowering profusely together. When nearing the top of the slope a narrow crossing path is met and you turn right along it. The route follows the lip of the valley where pretty field roses flower among the scrub. Just before this well trodden path enters woodland, and with a stone marker post on your left, bear right and continue along the valley edge. At a second stone marker post turn leftwards and continue along the narrow path. During early summer you will see large quantities of orchids flowering quite freely on these grassy slopes. Press on ahead until a T-junction is met where you should now turn right. Keep ahead on this broad track as it at first passes through trees before crossing a meadow to reach an information board by the parking area. Turn left here along Fox Lane to soon reach the Fox public house and the end of the walk.

PLACE OF INTEREST NEARBY
Honeywood Heritage Centre, a 17th century listed building alongside the picturesque ponds in Carshalton, off the A232 west of Croydon, contains displays on many aspects of the history of Sutton and a constantly changing programme of exhibitions on a wide range of subjects. Telephone 020 8770 4297.

GODSTONE, TILBURSTOW HILL AND BLETCHINGLEY

– *field paths and fine prospects*

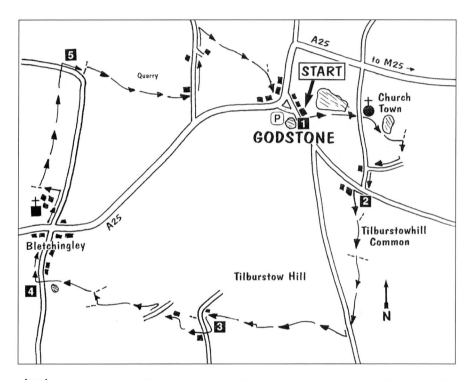

*T*his is a great walk for any time of the year. Starting in Godstone by the village pond, the route passes two more pretty ponds – one a nature reserve – before climbing steadily through woodland over Tilburstowhill Common. The way then continues along the foot of Tilburstow Hill where there are panoramic views across the Weald to the South Downs.

After reaching the old village of Bletchingley, the return route is along field paths, again with fine vistas. Many woodland and hedgerow birds and flowers can be seen on this varied ramble. Near the beginning there is one hill of note which is long rather than steep.

THE WALK

1 When facing the White Hart, walk along the small lane immediately to the right of the pub. Within yards continue ahead on a tarmac path that leads you past Bay Pond, a Surrey Wildlife Trust nature reserve. From this path you will be able to see Canada geese, moorhens and mute swans as well as winter visitors like pochard and tufted duck. I have been lucky enough to get a good close-up view of a great crested grebe from this path as well as being treated to a low level flying display by a couple of cormorants. Cross a small lane at the end of this path and enter the churchyard of St Nicholas' church. Continue to the right of the church and along an avenue of lime trees to soon exit the churchyard. The path now continues through trees to another pond which during summer is adorned with countless yellow water lilies. Judging by the embankment we pass over, this pond is entirely man-made and like Bay Pond would have been created as a header pond for the 16th and 17th century watermills in the area. Press on along this path as it goes leftwards up a slope through a clearing. Turn right when the path ends alongside a low

STARTING POINT: At the 15th century White Hart which is in the centre of Godstone and opposite the village green and pond. The White Hart is a Beefeater Inn owned by Whitbread and there is a good selection of food including a children's menu. This is a very popular pub and restaurant and it is necessary to book a table if wishing to dine here. Telephone: 01883 742521.

HOW TO GET THERE: Godstone is 6 miles east of Redhill and ³/₄ mile south of junction 6 on the M25. The White Hart is just yards south of the small one-way system in the centre of Godstone.

Arriva Buses serve the area.

PARKING: Patrons of the White Hart may use the pub car park while they walk (please ask first). There is alternative parking opposite alongside the village pond.

LENGTH OF WALK: 6¹/₂ miles. Map: OS Landranger 187 Dorking, Reigate and Crawley area (GR 351515).

brick wall and continue along a field edge to reach a stile. Cross the stile and turn rightwards along a narrow driveway where you pass the entrance to Leigh Place. At a T-junction with a small road turn left along the road and pass the lovely 15th century Old Packhorse, formerly an inn.

2 After crossing Gibbs Brook a T-junction is met where you should turn rightwards for 30 yards before crossing the road and continuing on a path that runs along the left-hand wall of a cottage. The path now climbs steadily uphill through beautiful woodland that contains a good mix of chestnut, oak, birch and holly. In the shadier spots in this woodland look out for the wonderful mosses that grow on dead tree stumps. If you look closely you may see the tiny candle snuff fungus that looks very much like miniature stags' horns. Remain in a forward direction and ignore any side paths and eventually the path descends to reach a road. Maintain direction along the road for 80 yards before turning right on a bridleway between banks. This lovely track passes along the foot of Tilburstow Hill and during spring and summer is lined by germander speedwell, bugle, cuckoo flower and the ever present red campion. When a field gate is reached go right for 10 yards and then left to maintain your original direction through woodland to reach a small country lane alongside a sunken pill box.

3 Turn left and continue down the lane and ignore a stile to your right at a bend. When a lovely old timbered house is met turn right on a bridleway that passes to the right of it.

One fungus the rambler often comes across, if not by sight but by its foul smell, is the aptly named stinkhorn (Phallus impudicus). If seen early on its first day the cap is covered in black spores that emit the foul odour. Flies are attracted by the smell and therefore unwittingly spread the spores. Most of the spores have gone in this picture. The fungus's risqué shape led Charles Darwin's daughter to burn any she found lest they risk the innocence of her house maids. Puritan Victorian editors printed illustrations of the fungi upside down so as not to offend readers.

*G*reat burdock, photographed here in winter, is a tall wayside plant with leaves of huge proportions. The stems grow to around 1.5 m high and around the base the leaves grow up to 35 cm long. After their summer flowering period the dried flower heads, or burrs, are left on the plant all winter where the many hooks catch on passing animals thus dispersing their seeds. The plant is rich in vitamin C and the roots and leaves are used in medicines for skin diseases.

This bridleway zig-zags through a field and soon passes close to a house named Little Coldharbour that seems idyllically sited. When a road is met turn right and continue along the rising road for a short distance. At the crest of the hill turn sharply leftwards by a large oak tree and continue along a narrow path. If walking with young children or a dog off the lead, beware of a vertical drop to your left for a short distance here. Press on through trees to soon reach a handily placed seat that offers magnificent views across the Weald. Our way continues ahead down the slope through scrub and along a wide track. At the end of the field to your right, turn right on a footpath that soon narrows as it passes through scrub to meet a T-junction. Turn left here and proceed along this partially surfaced path to pass a small pond bordered by yellow flag in summer to reach a road.

4 Turn right and continue along the road to soon reach the centre of Bletchingley. Cross the busy A25 and continue ahead along Church Lane. Pass a modern housing development that sits reasonably well in this old village and turn leftwards on a path that goes along the side of a golf course. At the end of a rather manicured area of grass, turn right over a stile and continue down a slope along the edge of the golf course. When the narrow ribbon of trees to your left sweeps round to the right follow the path through them to cross a stile at a field edge. Continue over a series of stiles in a straight line to reach a country lane. Whilst not criticising our modern farming methods these fields do illustrate the monoculture brought about by spraying and 'improving'.

5 Turn right along the lane and soon when it bends right go left through posts and within yards turn right and continue along a broad track that runs along a field edge. To your left is a hedge that contains field maple which helps mask a large quarry. Many hedgerow birds including robins, wrens and the even smaller goldcrest will be seen hopping around in the branches. It is nice to see that the landowner has planted a hedge around the large field on the right. The thousands of plants being used contain a good mixture of hawthorn, oak, ash and beech saplings which rather goes to blow the old theory of dating the age of a field hedge by the number of species growing in it. Alongside the track will be seen great burdock. During spring you will be aware of its huge leaves, some around the base of the plant reaching 30 to 35 cm long. Keep to this track for 3/4 mile until it ends by a house at a country lane. Turn left along the lane and in 1/3 of a mile go rightwards over a stile in a hedge to enter a field. The route now goes diagonally right on a distinct path worn into the grass to meet another stile at the edge of woodland. Press on along a fenced path to reach a kissing gate. Cross an open meadow and pass through a second kissing gate where you should now turn right. Continue along a track that leads you between houses to reach Godstone village green. The White Hart and the end of the walk are directly ahead of you.

PLACE OF INTEREST NEARBY
Godstone Farm is just the place for young and old alike where everyone is encouraged to stroke and feed the animals. A nature trail and adventure playground are suitable for children of all ages. Open daily between 10 am and 6 pm Godstone Farm is situated 1/2 mile south of Godstone on Tilburstow Hill Road. Telephone: 01883 742546.

REIGATE HEATH, THE PILGRIMS' WAY AND BUCKLAND

– in the shadow of the Buckland Hills

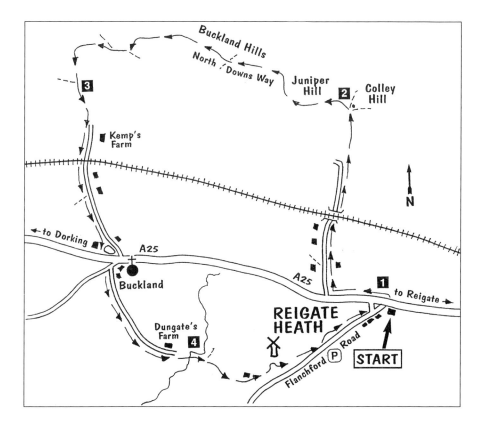

*T*his varied walk along the foot of the Buckland Hills is lovely at any time of year. The route offers panoramic rural views over the peaceful countryside that surrounds Buckland. In late spring and summer the wayside flowers include scabious, thyme, viper's bugloss and the more common varieties of orchid while in winter and early *spring the route is lined by dog's mercury, violets and lords and ladies. There is a good chance of spotting pheasants along the field edges while rabbits will be seen darting through the chalk scrub.*

Later the route passes the lovely village green at Buckland where a couple of seats offer a welcome rest while you admire the old tithe barn that makes the perfect backdrop to the village pond. The pond is covered in water lilies during summer and boasts carp 35 cm long.

THE WALK

1 From the Black Horse go left along the busy A25 in the direction of Dorking and quite soon turn right into Clintons Lane. This peaceful lane takes you away from the hurly burly of traffic speeding along the main road. The ivy that climbs up the mature trees around here is not a parasite as is commonly believed and will only compete for nourishment

STARTING POINT: At the Black Horse public house in West Street, Reigate, close to Reigate Heath. The pub serves Korean and Japanese food as well as a more traditional selection of English pub fare with children and vegetarians catered for. There is a pleasant garden and a children's play area is also available. Booking is advisable if you wish to dine here. Telephone 01737 245694.

HOW TO GET THERE: From junction 8 on the M25 head south for 1½ miles on the A217 to reach Reigate town centre. Take the A25 westward towards Dorking and in ¾ mile the Black Horse pub will be seen to your left. From Dorking take the A25 towards Reigate and soon after passing through Buckland the Black Horse pub will be seen to your right.

Arriva, Memory Lane and Tillingbourne Buses serve the area.

PARKING: Patrons of the Black Horse may use the pub car park while they walk (please ask first). There is alternative parking along Flanchford Road and a parking area a little further along the same road.

LENGTH OF WALK: 5½ miles. Map: OS Landranger 187 Dorking, Reigate and Crawley area (GR 243504).

with the host's roots. Although birds will be seen eating its berries they are poisonous to man even though in times of plague they were believed to be a cure. Ignore a footpath sign on your left and keep to the lane as it passes secluded houses in tranquil settings. Soon after passing the Old Manor House the route continues under a railway bridge. When the lane bends sharply leftwards press on ahead on a signposted path that continues along a narrow ribbon of trees. Fine views across the fields to Colley Hill and its castellated water tower are seen from this pretty path.

2 At the foot of Colley Hill by a junction of paths and a post turn left along a chalky narrower path that at first leads you through a hazel coppice. For the next 1½ miles this narrow path skirts the foot of the Buckland Hills and stays parallel to open fields. Eventually the hazel gives way to more open chalk hillside dotted with the small wayfaring tree. This tree has rather downy brown twigs and downy leaves especially on the underside. Flowering from late April to June the bunches of berries that follow turn black when ripe. Rabbits keep the grass closely cropped on these slopes and therefore unwittingly make the ideal habitat for orchids that flower here in early summer. At a junction of paths with steps to your right continue ahead along the North Downs Way. Soon, at a fork in the path by a post, continue along the left fork and later, after going down steps to a T-junction, turn right, again keeping on the North Downs Way. After passing a line of old yew trees on an incline watch out for another fork by a post. Go leftwards here on a downhill path through trees where you may spot a stinking iris or two. Soon the path continues between

Stinking iris or gladdon is a mainly woodland plant that grows to between one and two feet tall. The grey-purple flowers are seen in June and July and are followed by large seed heads that, during winter, split to display bright orange seeds. A folklore name for this plant is the roast beef plant due to the sickly sweet smell issued when crushed. This is more an indication of our ancestors eating decaying beef than anything else.

The wild teasel is a biennial which produces a rosette of prickly leaves in its first year followed by a tall flower stalk the next. The flowers open successively from the centre of the large conical flower-heads, both upwards and downwards. The fruiting heads are often dyed and used by flower arrangers. An earlier use for the plant was in the cloth industry where the flower-heads were used to raise or 'tease' the nap in newly woven cloth. The common name 'teasel' is derived from this use and the plant was once grown commercially near clothmaking mills.

fences across a field to reach a gate. You now leave the North Downs Way by pressing on through a field gate ahead of you and pass a large single oak tree in the field.

3 From this oak tree continue diagonally leftwards on a cart track to reach a second gate which you go through. Proceed along the farm track which soon becomes a tarmac drive and pass Kemp's Farm. With caution, re-cross the railway at the unmanned crossing and continue along this pleasant lane where clumps of teasel and great burdock (*see Walk 7*) are to be found. Eventually the lane meets Buckland village green where the route passes between the pond and old tithe barn to reach the A25. If it wasn't for the roar of traffic this spot would be idyllic. Cross with care to Old Road opposite and then go left into Dungate's Lane. After passing a couple of houses the banks on each side of the lane have herb Robert (*see Walk 14*) and other small flowers such as red campion and stitchwort amongst the grasses during summer. Keep on this quiet lane until it ends alongside the now gentrified Dungate's Farm. My mother and aunts lived here as children in the 1920s when it was then a working farm and a hive of activity. Unfortunately most of the fields have now been swallowed up by the ever increasing size of the sand pit on its doorstep. Press on along the farm track ahead that soon crosses and follows the Shag Brook for a few yards.

4 When the brook bends leftwards, continue ahead through a gate on a path signposted GW (Greensands Way) and cross a field. Pass through a second gate and continue along a farm track. Ahead you will notice Reigate Heath windmill. This 200 year old post mill forms what must be one of England's most unusual churches. Milling ceased in 1868 and by 1880 the roundhouse was in use as a church. When this track ends by a house and with a golf course ahead of you, press on ahead over a fairway to a sandy path opposite where the habitat suddenly changes to heathland dotted with Scots pine. Continue up a rise and then bear left and in 10 yards turn right. Very soon turn left again to continue along a sandy path that stays parallel to a road. The path eventually meets Flanchford Road where you keep ahead for 10 yards or so before bearing left onto a bridleway that remains parallel to the road. Soon the green is reached where you press on ahead to meet the Black Horse pub and the end of the walk.

PLACE OF INTEREST NEARBY

Polesden Lacey, sitting on the North Downs, is a beautiful Regency villa much altered in the early part of the 20th century. Once owned by Mrs Ronald Greville, a hostess known for her lavish house parties, the house is now in the hands of the National Trust. There is a fine collection of paintings, furniture, silver and porcelain on display as well as extensive gardens. Open from the end of March to the end of October daily except Mondays and Tuesdays, from 1.30 pm to 5.30 pm (open bank holidays). The gardens are open daily throughout the year from 11 am to dusk. Polesden Lacey is located off the A246, 2 miles south of Great Bookham. Telephone: 01372 458203.

BROCKHAM AND BETCHWORTH
– *river and parkland vistas*

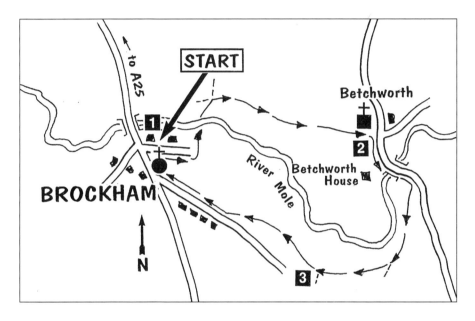

*T*his easy walk along field paths starts at one of Surrey's prettiest village greens and the scene of one of the county's largest Guy Fawkes bonfires. The masses that attend the celebration fail to spoil the centrepiece of Brockham as the green with its many charming houses, village water pump and attractively situated church soon recover and make a most agreeable sight.

Within yards of the start the route crosses the river Mole where it is possible to spot the occasional kingfisher darting above the water. During summer the heady scent of Himalayan balsam is caught on the breeze from the tall plants that grow along the river bank for part of its course. The turning point of the ramble comes as our way passes lovely Betchworth House, built in 1625. Soon the route re-crosses the Mole and climbs easily through open fields where you will have panoramic views across the meandering river to the North Downs.

THE WALK

1 When facing the Duke's Head, turn right and go to the end of the road by gates. The gate to the right is the 18th century village pound, now restored. The way is through the left-hand gate and along a bridleway that passes by a large ash tree. Cross the river Mole that is bordered here by Himalayan balsam and continue rightwards up a cart track lined with mature holly trees. At the top, by a junction of paths, turn right along a path that initially skirts the rear of gardens. On both sides of this path, including in a couple of the gardens, small shrub-like spindle trees will be seen. The name comes from its former use for making spindles for wool-spinning and as butchers' skewers. The twigs also make fine drawing charcoal and the French name for the tree, *fusain*, also means charcoal. During early summer the small green flowers are profuse but quite insignificant. The tree really comes to the fore

STARTING POINT: At the wonderful village green at Brockham that is blessed by two pubs, one of which is the Duke's Head, owned by the Allied Domecq brewery. Call in on the right day during summer and you will be entertained by morris dancers who make regular visits. The pub offers a good selection of beers and plenty of good pub food with choices for children

and vegetarians. Booking is not required. There is a garden, patio and children's play area for your enjoyment on warm summer days. Telephone: 01737 842023.

HOW TO GET THERE: From Dorking take the A25 east towards Reigate. In 1¹/₂ miles turn right on a road signposted to Brockham and soon after crossing the river Mole the green is reached. From Reigate take the A25 west towards Dorking. The turning to Brockham is on the left after 4 miles.
   Arriva, Memory Lane and Tillingbourne Buses serve the village.

PARKING: Patrons, with prior permission, may leave their cars at the Duke's Head while they walk or could park along the road by the village green or in Wheelers Lane by the church.

LENGTH OF WALK: 2¹/₄ miles. Map: OS Landranger 187 Dorking, Reigate and Crawley area (GR 198495).

during October and November when it is more easily spotted because of its vivid magenta four-lobed seed pods that split open to reveal bright orange sticky seeds. Press on along this path as it first goes along a field edge and then through gates, passing a farm along the way. Eventually the path reaches the churchyard of 13th century St Michael's church, now much restored. Continue along the waymarked path to exit the churchyard alongside Priest Cottage.

2 Turn immediately right here and continue along a raised pathway alongside the high walls of Betchworth House. Press on over the river Mole where you may be lucky enough to spot a kingfisher and after 30 yards cross a stile on your right. Proceed across the field and through a small coppice on the waymarked path where you will notice one or two wild cherry trees. Go over a small bridge and continue up a rise through the trees. Cross a stile at the top and carry on rightwards along a field edge. At the end of scrub on your right press on ahead, following a line of old oak trees along the crest of a ridge. Once the acorns, or mast, of the oak were highly valued by villagers as a source of food for their pigs and before the enclosure acts of the late 18th century they had rights of common pannage – pasturage for pigs. When the Domesday Book was written in 1086 a person's wealth in woodland was measured by the amount of pigs it could support. From this vantage point you have panoramic views across the parkland slopes to the river, Betchworth House and the North Downs beyond, while over to your left you will see Leith Hill in the distance.

Himalayan balsam, also known as policeman's helmet, is related to the impatiens (busy lizzie) family. This tall plant with hollow stems was originally grown in ornamental gardens but has now naturalised alongside streams and river banks. The strong scent, carried on the wind, is unmistakable. The flowers are rather orchid-like and when the ripe seed capsules are touched they explode which gives rise to yet another name, jumping jack.

The kingfisher is rather an oddly shaped bird with a large dagger-like beak and short stubby tail. It is shy and remains pretty much inconspicuous until it flies, then mostly you will only be aware of a flash of brilliant cobalt blue as it follows the course of a river. On spotting a stickleback or other such sized fish it will make a sudden dive and grasp it in its beak before making off to its perch where it will beat the fish to death before swallowing it head-first. The nest is usually at the end of a tunnel $^1/_2$ m to 1 m in length dug into the river bank. The nesting site can be recognised by a trail of foul-smelling slime running down from the entrance way.

3 At the end of this open area cross a stile and continue to the end of the field. Turn right and continue along the edge of woodland where pheasants will often be heard, to reach a third stile. Cross this and press on over a field diagonally half left to yet another stile which you cross. The route is now along the broad fenced track ahead of you where, after passing through a kissing gate, housing is reached at a road. Turn right along the road where you pass Brockham Primary School to reach the church on Brockham Green. Turn right here along a short path that brings you out to the green itself where you will see the Duke's Head pub ahead of you and the end of the walk.

PLACE OF INTEREST NEARBY
Gatwick Zoo and Aviaries is a children's zoo where all the family can have a good time. Donkeys, emus, wallabies, otters and meerkats plus tropical butterflies and birds are on show whilst large gardens, a lake and lawns combine to make the ideal picnic spot. Open all year from 10.30 am to 6 pm or dusk, the zoo is at Russ Hill near Charlwood, $4^1/_2$ miles south of Leigh. Telephone: 01293 862312.

WALK 10

THE RIVER WEY AND GODALMING NAVIGATIONS

– *idyllic towpath and watermeadows*

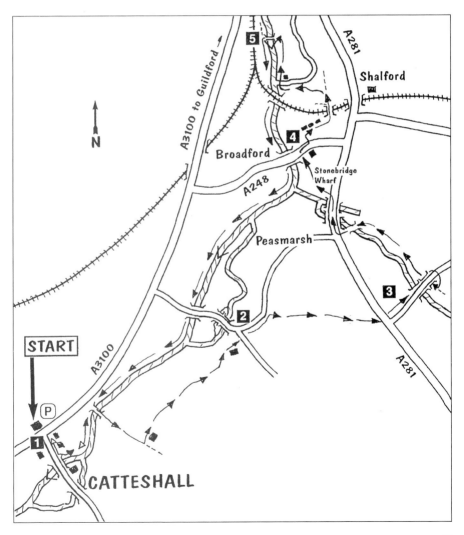

*T*his captivating walk is, for most of its way, along the towpaths of three canals. Near the start of the ramble you pass Farncombe Boathouse on the River Wey and Godalming Navigation, a popular spot where row boats and narrow boats are for hire. The route then continues alongside water-meadows to reach the now disused Wey and Arun Junction Canal where we link up with a section of the Wey South Path to reach Stonebridge Wharf. It was from this small wharf that locally made gunpowder was loaded onto narrow boats for shipment to London.

The route continues along the River Wey Navigation near Shalford as far as the Wey Valley Meadows – a Site of Special Scientific Interest – before returning to Godalming along the pretty towpath. Many interesting water plants and birds will be seen along the route. A shorter walk is available, returning from point 2 in the text, where only the Godalming Navigation is followed.

STARTING POINT: At the Leathern Bottle, a small and friendly pub in Meadrow not far from Godalming town centre. A good selection of wholesome food is available with a choice for vegetarians and children. There is a small and pleasant beer garden where on summer days you may wish to relax in the sun. Telephone: 01483 425642.

HOW TO GET THERE: The Leathern Bottle is in Meadrow (A3100) just ½ mile north-east of Godalming town centre. From Guildford take the A3100 and in 3½ miles the pub will be seen on your right next to a pay and display car park.

Tillingbourne Buses serve the area.

PARKING: Patrons of the Leathern Bottle may use the small pub car park while they walk (please ask first). There is additional parking in the pay and display car park next door (free on Sundays) or limited parking along Catteshall Road opposite.

LENGTH OF WALK: 2¼ or 6¾ miles. Map: OS Landranger 186 Aldershot, Guildford and surrounding area (GR 980448).

THE WALK

1 From the Leathern Bottle cross busy Meadrow and walk along Catteshall Road opposite. When the canal is reached by Farncombe Boathouse go left through a gate to reach the towpath where you continue along the pretty canal bank where lush marsh marigolds edge the water. When a brick bridge spanning the canal is reached you should turn right over it and press on along a farm track with water-meadows on your left. At a junction of tracks turn left on a bridleway and pass close to the side of a house where you continue to the left of stabling on a narrower fenced path between fields.

This path, lined variously by hawthorn, hazel, oak, ash and field maple, forms the boundary between the unimproved water-meadows on your left and the very much improved pasture on the right. The tiny wren makes its home along here and it will often be seen low down in a bush as it hunts for insects and spiders. Eventually this path meets a farm track where you maintain direction up a rise. Soon after this rise go left over a stile and cross another at a field edge. Go diagonally rightwards across the field and cross a stile to reach a small lane. Turn left here to meet a road junction.

Ragged Robin, a form of red campion, is one of the most characteristic flowers of low-land water-meadows during early summer. Standing 30 cm to 60 cm high the distinctively divided or 'ragged' petals are generally pink in colour or occasionally white. Although most reference books still state that ragged robin is common it is becoming increasingly scarce in Surrey due to more and more large-scale drainage programmes.

2 *For the shorter ramble you should turn left here and cross three road bridges to reach a gate on your left. Go through this gate and continue ahead along the towpath to reach Farncombe Boathouse where you retrace your steps back to the Leathern Bottle.* The longer ramble continues rightwards along Trunley Heath Road and 10 yards after passing the entrance to Unstead Manor turn right into a small lane alongside a Thames Water sign. The lane soon ends and you should

Canada geese were first brought to England as ornamental birds in the 15th century and by the 18th century were breeding quite freely in the wild. They are easily distinguished from other geese by their black neck and head with a broad white throat and cheek patch. They are fast in the air and flocks form in a V formation. The geese have one brood a year of five to six eggs that hatch in April or May.

continue ahead along a farm track where, on the left, it is pleasing to note that Thames Water are creating a large wetland nature reserve for the protection and enhancement of wildlife in the area. Press on along a narrower path between fields at the end of this track to soon meet a country lane. Cross this diagonally leftwards and maintain direction along a footpath. Continue over a driveway and press on ahead to reach the A281. Cross this busy road with care to the village green opposite and keep to the left edge, passing a pavilion with an interesting plaque to reach a quieter road.

3 Maintain direction ahead along the road and cross two road bridges. Immediately after the second bridge, turn sharply right on a path to meet the Wey South Path. Turn right again to pass under the bridge. The path now follows the bed of a disused railway that runs along the side of the defunct Wey and Arun Junction Canal. Press on along this pleasant path where there is every chance of seeing a green woodpecker or two flying between the trees. I was fortunate enough to spot, and get quite close to, a black redstart when passing this way. When the A281 is met, turn right along the road for a short distance before turning leftwards on a footpath next to a bridge parapet. This short path lined by holly trees leads you to housing where you go leftwards to soon meet the old Stonebridge Wharf at Broadford, once used for shipping the locally made gunpowder to London. Pass a modern office development that fits into the scene rather well and contrasts with the old wharf store sitting on steddles. Soon the road is reached.

4 Turn right along the road and when on a sharp bend alongside the Parrot public house cross to a small parking area by cottages. Go ahead and in 20 yards turn right along a footpath signposted to Shalford and Guildford. Maintain direction along an unmade road by cottages and ignore a right fork. At a junction of tracks press on ahead along a footpath signposted to Guildford where you soon cross a railway bridge. Ignore a footpath by the bridge and continue up a rise where you now turn left through a kissing gate. Go downhill on a stepped path to reach a planked walkway flanked by willow and alder trees as it takes you over a part of the water-meadows. At the bank of the river Wey turn left and pass more alder (*see Walk 3*) lining the bank with their roots dipping into the water. Cross a small weir to pass a picturesque cottage and continue along the bank of the Wey Navigation with the Wey Valley Meadows to your right. While a casual glance gives the impression that broom is the only plant here, don't be fooled as plenty of flowers are to be found including marsh orchid, marsh marigold, ragged robin and birdsfoot trefoil. Added to this are the large emerald butterfly, orange tipped butterfly, white admiral butterfly and the elephant hawk moth. In a short while the route reaches lock gates and the turning point of the ramble.

5 Cross the canal here and turn left along the towpath. The route now follows this side of the canal for 2½ miles where meadowsweet and purple loosestrife, both water-loving plants, abound as do moles so watch your footing. The canal bank offers more chances of seeing green woodpeckers as they dig up anthills in search of their staple diet of ants. You may also be treated to the spectacle of a flight of mute swans coming in to land on the still waters of the canal. Another bird that will be seen here is the Canada goose as it quite often feeds in large numbers on the adjoining fields. Soon after crossing a second road you will see, on the opposite bank, a pair of wizened crack willows. This tree is often planted alongside waterways as its roots help maintain the banks. The crack willow is so named because large twigs tend to crack off just above a joint and fall to the ground where they often propagate. Eventually the boathouse is reached where you may wish to visit the pretty tearooms where light refreshments are available throughout the summer and at weekends in winter. From here you should turn right and retrace your steps along Catteshall Road to meet the Leathern Bottle and the end of the walk.

PLACE OF INTEREST NEARBY
The Godalming Packetboat Company offers two-hour trips along the canal aboard the *Iona*, a traditional narrow boat pulled by one of their three heavy horses. All trips depart and return from Godalming Wharf near Sainsburys store. Telephone: 01483 425397.

SHACKLEFORD, GATWICK AND THE TARN

– *trees, heath and scenic ponds*

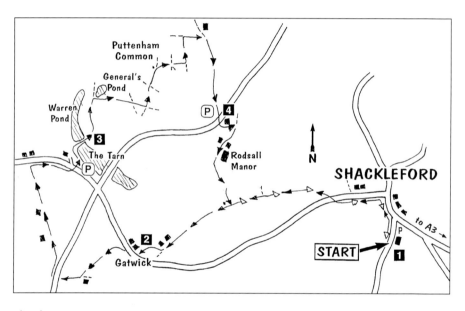

*T*his peaceful and varied walk starts in the small village of Shackleford before passing through oak, beech and hazel woodland to reach the tiny hamlet of Gatwick. Soon after this the habitat changes to heathland where the route continues over a causeway between Warren Pond and The Tarn. These beautiful ponds make a lovely picnic spot where you will see many water birds including great crested grebes.

The return journey takes you over Puttenham Common, an area measuring 470 acres and managed by Surrey County Council. The open heathland is a surviving fragment of what was once a huge tract of man-made landscape created by many centuries of clearance and grazing. Plenty of wayside plants including celandine, violets and the ever present red campion will be seen at most times of the year. The ramble contains one short, but steep ascent.

THE WALK

1 From the Cyder House Inn retrace your way back down the lane to the telephone box and bear left along The Street. Turn left into Lombard Street and pass Aldro School where a lovely old coach house dated 1743 now makes a handsome residence for the caretaker. Ignore a footpath on your right by a couple of houses and press on to another on your right in 200 yards or so. Cross a stile and the field ahead to another stile in the woodland edge. Maintain direction along a cart track through fine mixed woodland containing oak, beech and chestnut where, if you are lucky, you will spot the boldly patterned greater spotted woodpecker among the more common woodland birds. When the farm track bends sharply right press on ahead on a smaller sandy track. Ignore any side paths and keep to this easy downhill track until it reaches Kingshott Cottage. Turn right here on a signposted path where you soon meet a lane by Brookside Cottage in the peaceful hamlet of Gatwick.

STARTING POINT: At the Cyder House Inn in Pepperharrow Lane, Shackleford. This friendly, attractive little pub serves a wide selection of beer from the tap. There is a children's play area, patio and pleasant garden where you may have a relaxing lunch or summer evening meal. Booking is necessary at weekends if wishing to dine. Telephone: 01483 810360.

HOW TO GET THERE: Take the signposted road off the A3, 4¹/₂ miles south of Guildford, and follow the signs to Shackleford. As you enter the hamlet turn sharp left by a telephone box into Pepperharrow Lane. The pub is soon reached on your left.

Stagecoach Hants & Surrey Buses serve the area.

PARKING: Patrons of the Cyder House Inn may use the pub car park while they walk (please ask first) or alternatively you can avoid the sharp left-hand turn by the telephone box and park ahead of you alongside the road named The Street.

LENGTH OF WALK: 5¹/₂ miles. Map: OS Landranger 186 Aldershot, Guildford and surrounding area (GR 935453)

2 Turn right along the lane and after 150 yards bear left on a bridleway lined with holly. After crossing a stream go through a gate and cross a field to a second gate which you pass through. Turn right along the farm track to reach a road. Turn right along the road and soon by power cables bear left along a drive leading to Britty Hill Cottage. When the pretty boarded cottage is reached press on ahead, maintaining direction to eventually reach a road. Turn right along the road. Soon after passing a small road on your left you should turn left and go through a small parking area and make your way to the bank of The Tarn. Continue leftwards along the bank to reach a causeway and turn right to cross it. This area makes the perfect picnic spot where you can watch the many water birds that live here which include mute swans, wild ducks and coots. I have often seen great crested grebes here and if you are really lucky you may witness their fascinating head-shaking display.

3 At the end of the causeway continue up a slope and turn left on a wide path that follows a wire fence. After going over a boarded section of this path turn right by General's Pond. Continue along a path through a sea of bracken and at a crossing track press on ahead but at a second crossing track turn left. Continue ahead at a junction of paths and at a fork by a post keep to the right fork. At a large junction of tracks maintain direction ahead on a path that skirts the foot of hillocks. At a T-junction turn left and go up the rather sharp incline to a welcome seat. This seat offers an excellent vantage point where you may witness the occasional sparrowhawk (*see Walk 12*) on a hunting patrol overhead. Maintain direction and pass the seat to continue on a well defined path. The adder is a creature of these parts and can often be

The coot can easily be recognised by the pure white frontal shield and beak set against an almost pure black body. A more gregarious bird than the moorhen it can, if conditions are right, form quite sizeable flocks on large open stretches of water. It can be aggressive towards others of its kind and is often seen chasing them by scuttering across the water on its long greenish-coloured legs. The bird will be seen constantly diving below water where it can stay submerged for up to half a minute as it collects the weed that makes up the bulk of its diet.

The adder is Britain's only venomous snake and although its bite is serious it is not usually fatal to humans. The distinctive zig-zag pattern along its back and colouring make it almost invisible when basking in the morning sun around bracken. Being a type of viper means that its young are born live rather than hatched from eggs as other snakes. The young, usually about a dozen, are born during August and like their parents are deaf and can only make a quiet hiss. They hunt by sight and smell and live on mice, voles, frogs, slugs and small birds' eggs. During the winter months they hibernate, sometimes some distance from their summer hunting grounds.

seen basking in the early morning sun. Once it slithers into the bracken its zig-zag markings make it almost impossible to spot. Soon at a T-junction turn rightwards and continue along the wide sandy track. At another T-junction with a fence ahead of you turn right along a cart track which you now follow until a road is reached alongside a car park entrance.

4 Cross the road and pass the front of a house to reach a narrow footpath that goes to the right of it and alongside the garden. Within a short time the path goes steeply down to meet a sunken track where you should now turn right. Pass lovely Rose Cottage and by the end of the garden wall of Rodsall Manor turn left on a stony bridleway. Soon this path broadens and continues through mature woodland. It is not long before a T-junction is met by a post where you now turn left and continue up the rising sandy track walked earlier. At a junction of tracks press on ahead along the farm track. When the farm track bends to the right continue ahead over a stile and cross the field to retrace your steps back to the Cyder House Inn and the end of the walk.

PLACE OF INTEREST NEARBY
Loseley House was built in 1562 from the remains of Waverley Abbey for Sir William More and is still owned by Sir William's descendants. The house is set in magnificent parkland that is grazed by the Loseley Jersey Herd. The Walled Garden contains mulberry trees, herbaceous borders and herb gardens among other things. Loseley House is 3 miles west of Guildford off the B3000. Telephone: 01483 304440.

WALK 12

THE RIVER WEY AND FRENSHAM GREAT POND

– river, lake and country park

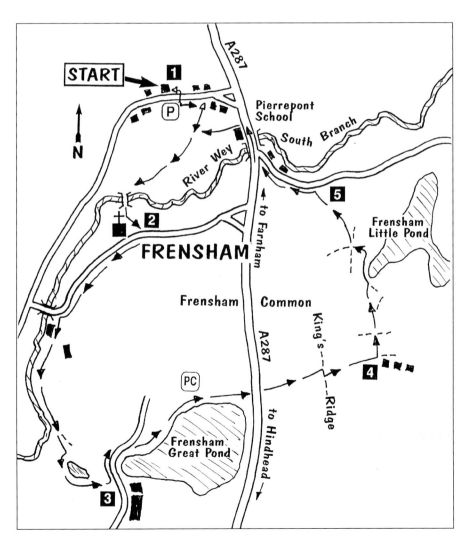

*T*his is a first-rate walk for any time of the year as there will always be something to see – a bright flash of blue as a kingfisher darts along the bank of the River Wey South Branch, a flock of geese landing on the waters of Frensham Great Pond or a sparrowhawk flying overhead in search of a meal.

After following the River Wey South Branch the route continues along the shore of Frensham Great Pond where reed warblers, great crested grebes, tufted ducks and herons make their home. Later the route crosses King's Ridge Barrows, a small group of Bronze Age burial mounds some 3,500 years old from where panoramic views across the whole of Frensham Common Nature Reserve can be seen. Woodlarks, silver studded blue butterflies and sand lizards are a feature of this wonderful heathland.

STARTING POINT: At the Holly Bush public house in Shortfield Road, Frensham. This welcoming pub, owned by the Morland Brewery, serves Ruddles Best Bitter, Bombadier and Old Speckled Hen beers from the tap with wine available by the glass or bottle. A good choice of pub food is on offer every day between 12 noon and 2 pm including a selection for  children. There is a children's play area and a pleasant garden and patio where you can relax in summer. Booking is advisable if wishing to lunch at this popular pub. Telephone: 01252 793593.

HOW TO GET THERE: From Farnham follow the A287 south for 2¹/₂ miles. After going up Gong Hill, Shortfield Road is third on your right. From Hindhead follow the A287 north for 6 miles and after passing the Mariners public house, Shortfield Road will be seen on your left. The Holly Bush public house is 100 yards past the cricket ground.
   Stagecoach Buses serve the area.

PARKING: With prior permission at the Holly Bush or alternative parking is available by the cricket ground.

LENGTH OF WALK: 4³/₄ miles. Map: OS Landranger 186 Aldershot, Guildford and surrounding area (GR 845422).

THE WALK

1 With your back to the Holly Bush pub turn left along the road to reach the cricket ground. Maintain direction inside the recreation area and at a line of pollarded trees turn right and continue along the boundary hedge. At the corner of the recreation ground ignore a downhill path and go right over a stile. Continue ahead along the left edge of a field and follow a distinct path as it passes through a couple of meadows. The River Wey South Branch will soon be seen meandering away to your left and with a bit of luck you may see a grey heron fishing for food. The path bends to the right along a field edge to eventually meet a small bridge. Go left over the bridge and continue along a very pleasant wide path that passes a graveyard and reaches a road alongside St Mary the Virgin church.

2 Turn right and continue along the road. Soon after passing the entrance gates to Frensham Manor the road turns right over the river. Keep ahead here on a bridleway through the wrought iron gates of the Mill House. This very pleasant track follows the river bank which makes the ideal place for kingfishers (*see Walk 9*) to create their nests and where on a good day you will see a flash of blue as one darts over the water in search small fish. One or two trees to your left often have mistletoe (*see Walk 17*) growing high in their branches. Leave the bridleway at a fork by a fingerpost and bear right on a narrower footpath that leads you to a secluded lake where willows and great reedmace are mirrored in the still waters. Cross a sluice on your right and follow the right-hand bank of the lake.

Great reedmace colonises the edges of ponds, lakes and slow moving rivers where the rhizomes live on the rich silt. After a time, the densely growing roots trap even more silt and detritus, thereby slowly raising the muddy bottom rather like mangroves do in the sea. The top part of the flower is male whilst the dark brown velvety fruiting spike is female. Dried reedmace leaves are used in basket making and the rhizomes can be roasted and used as a coffee substitute.

The sight of a sparrowhawk hunting is awesome. Its prey, often starlings, have very little chance of escape out in the open as the hawk flies fast and low with only three or four wing-beats between glides and can outfly all others. If its prey makes it to the trees the sparrowhawk's flying skills come to the fore as it threads its way between them at high speed. Once the prey has been caught in the sparrowhawk's strong talons it is often flown to a favourite plucking post or tree stump where it is then eaten.

I find that the peace and tranquillity of this sheltered place makes the ideal spot to spend a few moments observing the water birds as they go about their daily business. At the end of the lake press on ahead to soon reach a road by the Frensham Pond Hotel.

3 Turn left along the road and soon the open water of Frensham Great Pond comes into view. On a bend in the road go right on a bridleway that follows the bank of the lake and then continue ahead when the bridleway goes left up an incline. The flora and fauna now changes to that more in line with open heaths. Carry on along the shore-line of the lake which is fringed in places with great reedmace and finally reach the A287 alongside a bus stop. Cross the road to a track signposted with an orange marker arrow and maintain direction. The soft sandy soil here is especially suited to the tiny sand lizards that scurry around in the heat of the sun while above, the occasional woodlark will be seen. This quite scarce little bird can be distinguished from its more common relative the skylark by its shorter tail and its jerky undulating flight. Climb to the crest of a ridge known as King's Ridge from where most of the country park can be viewed. Turn rightwards here by an information board and in 50 yards turn left and continue downhill on a broad track to maintain your original direction.

4 About 50 yards before reaching a house follow the orange marker leftwards. The occasional sparrowhawk will be seen hunting around this area so keep your eyes peeled. Soon at a junction of tracks you should continue ahead. At a fork in the track ignore an orange marker pointing right and press on ahead. When a path is met by Frensham Little Pond turn left along it. Finally at a T-junction turn right on a wide sandy track. Keep to the left-hand of two tracks and soon pass a post inscribed with the number 520. Ignore any side paths and maintain direction on the soft sandy track that takes you through a fine stand of pines and brings you to a small parking area and a narrow lane.

5 Turn left and walk along this pleasant lane where you pass a couple of fine houses with pretty gardens backing onto the bank of the winding river Wey. When you reach the A287 once again, cross the road and turn right to reach the Mariners public house. Here you turn left on a narrow fenced path that runs along the right-hand side of the pub building and garden. Continue up a rise and at a junction of paths turn right into the cricket ground and retrace your steps back to the Holly Bush and the end of the walk.

PLACE OF INTEREST NEARBY
Farnham Castle Keep was used by the medieval bishops of Winchester and has been in continuous occupation since the 12th century. The shell-keep encloses a mound in which are the massive foundations of a Norman tower. The castle is open from 1st April to 1st November from 10 am to 6 pm or dusk and is situated in Castle Hill $^1/_2$ mile north of Farnham town centre on the A287. Telephone: 01252 713393.

WALK 13

ELSTEAD AND BAGMOOR COMMON NATURE RESERVE

– woodland glades and secretive pools

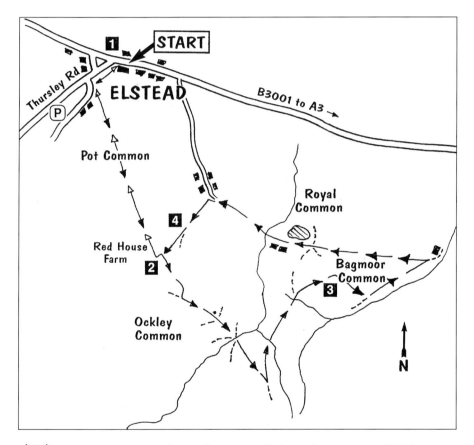

*T*his quiet and peaceful walk starts off through a series of fields across Pot Common that offer fine views over Elstead. The route then leads you through Bagmoor Common Nature Reserve. This area owned and managed by the Surrey Wildlife Trust was once open heath but is now covered by birch woodland with some pine and aspen. The quiet walker may see roe deer as well as sparrowhawks, woodcock, green woodpeckers

63

and the harder to spot adders, grass snakes and slow worms that all live here.

If you walk with a dog as I do, please keep it on a leash whilst on the reserve. This will not only help protect wildlife, but also the dog itself as it may be bitten by a startled adder. Humans, however, have nothing to fear as the snakes will avoid you by sensing the vibrations from your footsteps long before you arrive. The return journey passes a small idyllic lake that makes a perfect picnic spot for those wishing to spend more time in this captivating area.

THE WALK

1 From the Woolpack go left to the small triangular village green and continue leftwards, passing a doctor's surgery. Turn into Stacey's Farm Road where you continue immediately leftwards up a fenced footpath. At the top of the incline cross a stile and continue ahead to a

STARTING POINT: At the Woolpack public house by the small green which forms the core of Elstead. The aptly named 16th century pub was originally a store for fleeces in what was once an area dominated by sheep farming and the wool industry. A good variety of food is on offer and there is a garden and children's play area for use when the weather permits. Telephone: 01252 703106.

HOW TO GET THERE: Elstead is situated on the B3001, 2 miles west of the A3 at Milford. The Woolpack is in the centre of the village a few yards away from the village green.
  Tillingbourne Buses serve the area.

PARKING: Patrons of the Woolpack may use the pub car park while they walk (please ask first). There is alternative parking along Thursley Road by the green and a little further along the same road is a layby.

LENGTH OF WALK: 5 miles. Map: OS Landranger 186 Aldershot, Guildford and surrounding area (GR 908437).

second stile. Maintain direction ahead on a fenced path between fields to reach a third stile where you press on along the right-hand field edge. At the end of this large field maintain direction on a farm track. Continue over another stile and follow the field edge. At the end of this field go leftwards for 50 yards and then cross a stile on your right. Continuing along the right-hand field edge brings you to woodland.

2 Ignore a stile on your right and press on ahead, maintaining direction through pleasant birch and pine woodland where soon the path becomes sandy and the vista changes to heathland. At a forestry track press on ahead along it and soon after passing under power cables at a junction of paths by a post, maintain direction. At a second junction of paths by a post bear right along a broad track and in 150 yards by an English Nature Reserve sign turn leftwards. Keep left at a fork and pass through a stand of Scots pine to soon reach a T-junction by another English Nature sign. Turn left here and soon after crossing a small brook turn right on a footpath by a post. Pass to the right of a small man-made knoll where the path now runs parallel to power cables. Closer inspection of the young oak trees around here will reveal the occasional oak gall.

Oak galls are caused by gall wasps that lay their eggs on the oak tree. This then induces the tree into forming an abnormal growth or gall around the larvae thereby unwittingly protecting them from predators. Here you can see the bore holes of the escaping infant gall wasps, also known as gallflies. Oak trees offer more shelter and food to wildlife than any other of our native trees. It has been catalogued that up to 300 different species of insect and small animal make use of the flowers, leaves, fruit, bark and roots of the tree. Added to this are the small birds, squirrels, dormice, wood mice and wood pigeons that, in turn, feed on them.

3 At a Ministry of Defence warning sign bear right and keep to the main path where you now enter the Surrey Wildlife Trust nature reserve. At a T-junction turn leftwards and continue along the well defined path. There is a small stream through the trees to your right where dragonflies patrol and the occasional kingfisher darts (*see Walks 18 and 19*). At a line of power cables 50 yards before reaching a house turn sharply left and continue through posts.

The path now follows the power cables and after a while becomes less distinct. The bracken around this area harbours the rather solitary woodcock where its beautiful markings of buff, rich brown and black camouflage it perfectly. Another creature camouflaged by the bracken is the adder (*see Walk 11*) and if you are here early you may well see one in the distance basking in the morning sun. When the power cables go rightwards press on ahead to reach the tranquil waters of a small lake. Our route continues ahead along the left side of the lake where you soon pass a couple of houses aptly named Pond Cottages. Pass through this idyllic setting and continue along a driveway. At the end of the drive by a gate and housing turn left on a broad public bridleway bordered by holly.

4 Ignore a left fork by a Ministry of Defence sign and keep ahead. Disregard a stile on your right and press on alongside a field. At the end of the field, by another Ministry of Defence sign, you should turn right over a stile and retrace your steps back through the series of very pleasant fields to reach the Woolpack and the end of the walk.

PLACE OF INTEREST NEARBY
Birdworld and Underwater World will provide an enjoyable day out for all the family. The owner has turned his hobby of keeping exotic birds and fish successfully into his profession and his enthusiasm is shown in the well produced guide book. Open all year round – check times – the attraction will be found at Holt Pound, 1 mile south of Farnham on the A325. Telephone: 01420 22140.

WALK 14

BLACKHEATH AND FARLEY GREEN

– sunken paths and sandy tracks

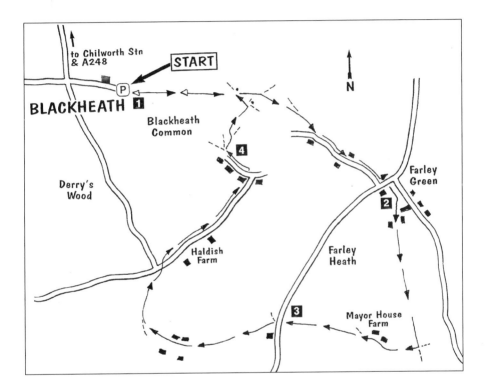

*T*his appealing walk starts at Blackheath Common, an SSSI where the combination of heathland and pine woodland not only suits sand lizards but many ground nesting birds such as woodlark and nightjar. Nightjars are nocturnal birds spending the day sitting immobile in trees or on the ground and are very well camouflaged and hard to spot. Green woodpeckers, goldcrests and long tailed tits are also regular visitors here so the observant rambler will have plenty to look out for throughout the year. Later on the route passes along sunken tracks where the high sandy banks are alive with wild flowers and small burrowing creatures.

THE WALK

1 Take the broad sandy bridleway through pine trees that continues on from the lane you have just travelled. Ignore all crossing tracks and keep ahead on the main track as it passes through peaceful pine and birch woodland. After ³/₄ mile when a definite fork in the main track is reached bear right. Within yards the vista changes and you pass a wide clearing surrounded by silver birch trees. Keep ahead on a sandy track and in 150 yards another path comes in from the left by a seat. Bear right here and press on downhill to soon meet a small unmade farm track by Lipscombe Cottage. Continue leftwards, passing a couple of houses, one appropriately named 'Ramblers'. When this track meets August Lane, turn left and continue along the lane to reach the triangular green at Farley Green.

2 At the small green bear right and continue on a sandy track that keeps to the right of the green. Follow the track as it leaves the village green behind and passes to the right of a large house. Soon the track goes between a smaller house named The Cottage and a barn.

STARTING POINT: At the parking area in Blackheath Lane a few yards past the Villagers public house. This country pub offers a wide selection of food from the children's, vegetarian and à la carte menus. This is a popular pub at weekends and if wishing to dine booking is recommended. Telephone: 01483 893152.

HOW TO GET THERE: Turn off the A248 at Chilworth by the station and go over the level crossing. Press along the small lane until a crossroads is reached where you should turn left. Pass the Villagers public house to reach the parking area from where the ramble starts.

Tillingbourne Buses and Thames Trains serve the Chilworth area.

PARKING: In the parking area just past the Villagers public house.

LENGTH OF WALK: 5³/₄ miles. Map: OS Landranger 186 Aldershot, Guildford and surrounding area and 187 Dorking, Reigate and Crawley area (GR 037461).

Known as Ride Lane, this deeply eroded track soon continues below field level and its high sandy banks bring the plants that grow here up to eye level. For most of the year you will see lords and ladies growing on these sheltered banks which offer a frost free environment during their early springtime flowering. The sheath soon gives way to a stout stem bearing 20 to 30 berries that at first are green before becoming bright red. When a large crossing track is reached, turn right and continue along a wider, slowly rising sunken track. After passing stables and Mayor House Farm the track bends to the right and soon meets a fork. Ignore the right fork and remain on the main farm track until a small country road is eventually reached.

3 Cross to a bridleway opposite, ignoring one to your right. This attractive track follows the crest of a ridge and offers outstanding views across the surrounding countryside. Quite often jays are present around here and you will more likely hear their sharp warning cry as you approach rather than see them as they are extremely shy and remain hidden in the trees. They are the most colourful member of the crow family but unfortunately are much persecuted by gamekeepers as they are habitual egg thieves. After passing two large barns and a couple of houses the track narrows and goes downhill. At a junction of paths bear right and continue downhill, again between high banks, to reach a narrow lane. Turn right here and walk along the road,

In late winter the young shoots of lords and ladies or cuckoo-pint as it is also called are just visible and at this stage look very like young tulip shoots. When these plants flower in April and May the sheath contains male and female flowers below a hairy structure. Small dung midges, enticed by the bad odour the plant gives out, fall into this trap and are not released until they have pollinated the female flowers, at which time the hairs wither, enabling them to make their escape. Later in the year the rest of the plant withers away, leaving upright spikes of green berries that later turn bright red and are highly poisonous.

Herb Robert, seen here flowering in June, is thought to be named after a French Cistercian monk, Abbot Robert. Herb Robert is part of the geranium family and is remarkable for the number of common names it is known by, Jenny Wren, dog's toe, dragon's blood and poor Robin (after Robin redbreast) to name but a few. The latter two names reflect the fact that the leaves and stems often turn bright red later in the season. The delicate pink flowers have white streaks lengthwise and grow in pairs. In folk medicine the fresh stems were used to heal wounds.

passing Haldish Farm. The banks on either side are decorated with the delicate little herb Robert and more lords and ladies. At a T-junction alongside a small converted barn with a moss-covered roof turn left along a narrow lane.

4 Soon the lane ends by a cottage and a 'Hurtwood Control' sign. Bear right here and in 10 yards at a second fork bear right again. About 50 yards further on at yet another fork, keep to the left and maintain direction ahead. The track goes through birch and pine trees as it leads you back over Blackheath. Stay on the main track ignoring small paths to either side. After following a low bank the track meets a crossing track by a post. Turn left here and in a short while you come to another crossing track and post. Turn left again and retrace your steps along this wide track until the parking area and the end of the walk are reached.

PLACE OF INTEREST NEARBY

Shalford Mill is owned by the National Trust and is prettily situated astride the Tilling Bourne at Shalford. Built in the early 18th century the tile-hung building still retains its machinery which last worked in 1914. Open daily from 9 am to 5 pm the mill is 1 mile south of Guildford on the A281. Telephone: 01483 561617.

WALK 15

FRIDAY STREET, ABINGER BOTTOM AND LEITH HILL

– enchanting woodland and panoramic views

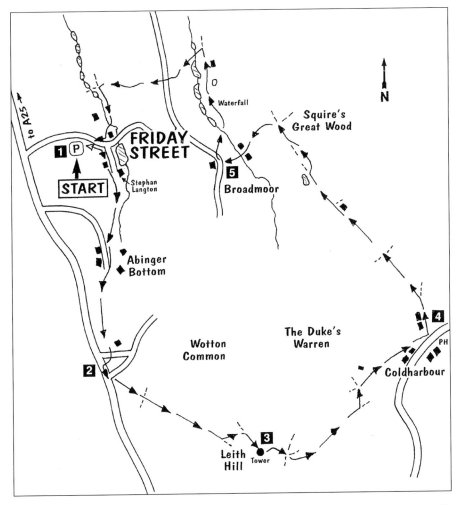

*I*n his 1938 book in 'The King's England' series Arthur Mee describes Friday Street as having 'the sound of falling water and the sight of Nature at her best'. This still holds true today as this magnificent walk through peaceful woodland proves. Although never far from human habitation, very little sign of it is to be seen from these tranquil woodland tracks. After leaving the old hammer pond behind at Friday Street the route follows a pretty stream through open beech woodland on a track that climbs gradually up the northern flank of Leith Hill. When Leith Hill Tower is reached, panoramic views across the Weald to the South Downs and Chanctonbury Ring are there to delight the eye.

The return journey touches the edge of Coldharbour before turning and passing through more wonderful woodland to reach the small hamlet of Broadmoor. For a while the route follows another small stream and passes a waterfall before crossing a valley and returning to Friday Street. Roe

STARTING POINT: At a parking area just outside Friday Street as parking by the Stephan Langton Inn and Restaurant can be a lottery. There has been a pub on this site since the 17th century but this building replaced the earlier one after a disastrous fire in the 1930s. The pub is named after the 13th century Archbishop of Canterbury who presided over the signing of the Magna Carta. Although the pub has no garden there is a pleasant patio area where you can soak up the country air. Telephone: 01306 730775.

HOW TO GET THERE: Turn off the A25, 2 miles west of Dorking, on a small road signposted to Friday Street. After approximately 1 mile watch out for a very sharp left turn into a small lane again signposted to Friday Street. Abinger Common free car park will soon be met on your right.

No public transport serves this quiet hamlet.

PARKING: Very limited at the Stephan Langton. No parking at all in Friday Street but plenty of room in the free car park where the ramble starts.

LENGTH OF WALK: $6\frac{1}{4}$ miles. Map: OS Landranger 187 Dorking, Reigate and Crawley area (GR 126458).

deer, pheasants and many woodland birds and plants will be seen on this lovely circuit. The ramble contains one short but quite steep ascent and one fairly steep descent.

THE WALK

1 From the corner of the free car park continue downhill alongside the road in the direction of Friday Street to soon meet the old hammer pond. Turn right here and walk along the lane to pass the Stephan Langton public house and restaurant. When the lane ends press on ahead on a wide track that continues up the valley floor. This track is a delight no matter what time of year you pass along it but it is possibly at its best when the beech trees are showing their autumnal colours. The small stream to your left feeds the hammer pond before joining with another to form the Tilling Bourne. Quite often roe deer will be seen in this woodland as well as many woodland birds such as the chaffinch. This is our commonest finch and like most other birds the male is the more colourful. During winter this charming bird is often seen in the company of bramblings, winter visitors from Siberia. Ignore any side paths and when a lane is reached at the hamlet of Abinger Bottom turn leftwards along it for a short distance. Quite soon when the lane turns leftwards you should continue ahead along a bridleway. Maintain direction on the main track and at a fork bear right. Soon cross a lane and press on to reach a road.

2 Turn left along the road for a short distance to reach a road junction where you should now go diagonally left and continue along a

A burr, as shown here on the trunk of this old oak tree, is generally caused by an injury through careless tree felling early on in the tree's life. The area affected has since been growing in a disordered way, resulting in these large lumps or burrs. The wood from burr-oak and burr-walnut is expensive and much prized by cabinet makers who use the unusual grain pattern for veneers.

*R*oe deer, unlike their larger cousins in Richmond Park, are quite small and are about the size of a large dog. Although not too numerous they are widespread throughout Surrey. The male and female are easily distinguished by their white rump patches, an inverted heart shape for the female and kidney shaped for the male. The male grows 'velvet' antlers which it sheds each year. When first born the young have light patches on their coats that help to camouflage them in dappled sunlight.

bridleway through more woodland, this time predominantly pine. Ignore a crossing track and maintain direction. Later, ignore a wide track to your left but in 50 yards at a junction of tracks, continue ahead on a narrower path. In about 150 yards at a fork, take a smaller path leftwards. This quite pitted path soon brings you to a T-junction where you should now turn right and remain in this direction to soon reach the top of Leith Hill alongside Leith Hill Tower. There are plenty of picnic tables here so that you can rest and enjoy the magnificent views.

3 Facing the escarpment and with the tower immediately behind you go left on a broad downhill track. At a large junction of tracks at the foot of this hill continue diagonally right on an uphill path where in 30 yards you should bear right at a fork. Soon at another junction of paths go forward to pass low posts and then turn leftwards on a lovely path that follows the edge of the escarpment. Continue on this pleasant path as it passes under scented pine trees with an undercover of bilberry. Follow the marker posts with green direction arrows to eventually reach Coldharbour cricket pitch. Leaving the marker posts behind, the route now goes rightwards along the wide track that after passing the cricket pitch continues downhill to reach the edge of Coldharbour village – at 750 feet above sea level the highest village in Surrey.

4 Turn left on a bridleway opposite the Plough Inn and pass a couple of well placed houses before re-entering mixed woodland. At a junction of tracks press on along the left fork ahead of you. Stay on this easy track as it goes through quiet woodland and soon after passing the ruins of a cottage ignore paths to left and right. At a small woodland pool the track divides and it is best to keep to the right fork. About 250 yards after the left fork rejoins the route you should turn left at a junction of paths. This path is lined by laurel and holly bushes and descends into the valley below alongside a picturesque cottage in the hamlet of Broadmoor. Press on ahead along the drive and bear right on a path to soon meet another drive. Continue along this for a few yards to reach a road by riding stables.

5 Turn right along the road for 50 yards before bearing right on a footpath along a broad track. This path follows the valley floor where the second stream that makes up the Tilling Bourne tumbles over a waterfall to feed a series of small ponds in the fields to your left. These water features are not in the least bit natural but do help to create a more diverse habitat for wildlife. Not long after passing a house in a secluded setting you should turn left over a stile and pass between two of these ponds to reach a stile. The path now goes rightwards steeply uphill for a short distance to reach a road which you cross. Continue ahead on the path opposite and at a junction of paths by a wire fence press on ahead along the grassy track. Eventually the path goes steeply downhill to a stile by a junction of tracks and two more ponds. Turn left here and soon pass picturesque Yew Tree Cottage where at a fork in the track you should bear right. Soon you cross a ford and pass a meadow where quite often a dozen or so rabbits will be seen grazing. Within yards the hammer pond at Friday Street is reached where the Stephan Langton pub and restaurant can be found along the lane directly ahead of you while the car park and the end of the walk are along the lane to your right.

PLACE OF INTEREST NEARBY

Leith Hill Tower was built back in 1766 by Richard Hull. It is thought that he built the tower to raise the level of Leith Hill to 1,000 feet above sea level. Later additions in 1788 and during Victorian times mean that the top is now 29 feet higher and is certainly the highest place in south-east England. Richard Hull is buried beneath the tower and tradition has it that he had himself interred upside down in his belief that the world would turn on its axis and he 'wished to stand before his Maker right way up'.

WALK 16

OUTWOOD AND WASP GREEN

– *hornbeam and hedgerows*

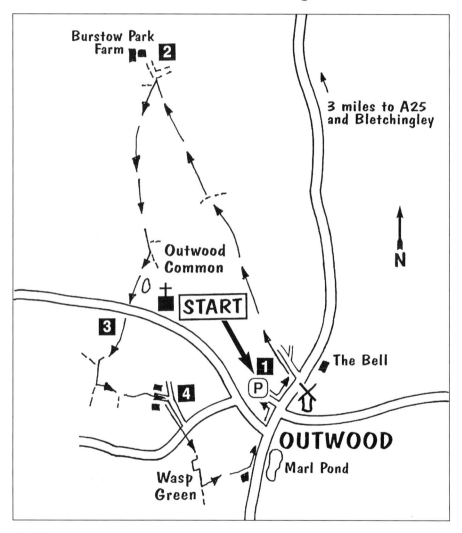

*T*his is a lovely walk for any time of the year. It starts opposite the famous Outwood windmill which was built in 1665. The mill has been expertly restored and is open to the public at certain times of the *year. Interestingly, another mill was built alongside in 1800 with the intention of supplanting it but by the early part of the 20th century it was in a state of disrepair and finally collapsed in 1962. The route passes through mixed woodland and open farmland that form part of the Harewood Estate, an area covering some 2,500 acres. The superb oak woodland along the route also contains hornbeam, much valued for its fine charcoal.*

During winter you have every chance of seeing green woodpeckers, fieldfares, rabbits and the occasional hare while in spring and summer the woodland is carpeted by swathes of bluebell and wood anemone. All year round the hedgerows are alive with robins, tits and wrens that live in the dense hawthorn while in the sky above skylarks can be heard.

THE WALK

1 From the National Trust car park walk back to Outwood Road and turn left and soon turn left again along a small lane. If starting from the Bell pub walk uphill to reach the green and turn right along the small lane. After passing a couple of houses and Windmill Garage keep ahead and left at a fork and when the lane abruptly ends by a house,

STARTING POINT: At the National Trust parking area to the south of the Bell public house. Booking is essential if wishing to dine at this popular pub at weekends or bank holidays. Telephone: 01342 842989.

HOW TO GET THERE: Turn off the A25 at Bletchingley and head south along Outwood Lane. After 3 miles the Bell public house will be seen to your left while a little further on opposite the windmill – second on the right – is the National Trust parking area.

Cruisers and Post Office Postbuses serve the area

PARKING: In the National Trust parking area opposite the windmill or at the Bell, with prior permission, patrons only.

LENGTH OF WALK: 4$^1/_2$ miles. Map: OS Landranger 187 Dorking, Reigate and Crawley area (GR 327456).

appropriately named Path End, maintain direction. Cross a stile and enter a field, again keeping ahead. At a second field ignore a path on your left and maintain direction along the right-hand field edge. Whilst walking this way last I was fortunate enough to see a hare running across the fields. Although books will inform you that hares are common, I don't believe their numbers are great in Surrey at all as they are much more suited to the prairie-style farming of East Anglia. A series of stiles and

Hawthorn is a common shrub throughout Britain and as such has attracted much folklore. The name is derived from the old English word 'hawe' which meant a space enclosed by a hedge – the most common use for the plant. One of the legends surrounding hawthorn concerns the Holy Thorn of Glastonbury which it is said sprang from the staff of Joseph of Arimathea on his return from the Holy Land. His staff was reputedly an offshoot of Christ's Crown of Thorns. The berries can be steeped in brandy to make liqueur or they can be mixed with crab apples to make a tasty jelly. Culpeper, the 17th century herbalist, wrote that 'the seeds in the berries, beaten to powder, being drunk in wine are held singularly good against the stone'. To complete the plant's versatility the young leaves can be eaten in salads and the flower buds used to make a pudding giving rise to one of the shrub's odder names, Chucky Cheese. Haws are an important source of food for birds and small mammals and 23 species have been recorded as eating them.

fields follow that will bring you to a farm track by Burstow Park Farm.

2 Turn immediately left here on a bridleway and ignore a right turn in 10 yards. At a small brook go through a field gate and continue ahead to meet two gates alongside each other. Proceed through the right-hand gate and continue in the same direction. During winter it is possible to spot a small flock of fieldfares visiting from Scandinavia. They are a part of the thrush family and prefer to forage in open fields for worms and insects than in woodland. Soon the bridleway becomes enclosed and some 200 yards after entering mixed woodland you should turn right by a post. Pass a small pond with a welcoming seat – an ideal picnic spot – and ignore a path on your left. Soon the route meets a road which you cross to a public footpath opposite.

3 Continue along this fenced path and cross a small brook and a stile. Press on ahead and 30 yards before the end of the field go left over a stile. Continue along a hedgerow on the right-hand field edge to reach a junction of paths and two stiles. Ignore the stile on your right and cross the stile ahead and continue over the field to another stile alongside a field gate. Cross this stile and press on between a bungalow and farm buildings to reach a driveway and eventually a road.

4 Turn right along the road and in a few yards at a T-junction press on ahead on a public footpath. Keep to the waymarked path as it zig-zags across a small brook via two stiles. Continue ahead over a third stile and 70 yards before another stile is reached turn left over a stile and walk through a small plantation of trees. The path ends alongside a lovely house and opposite a small lake, once an old marlpit. Marl is a calcareous mudstone that was spread on poor soil to fertilise it and reduce its acidity. Turn left along the road to soon meet Outwood village green, the windmill and the end of the walk.

PLACE OF INTEREST NEARBY
Outwood Post Mill is the oldest working windmill in England. Built way back in 1665 the mill has a black weather-boarded body surmounting a single storey brick roundhouse. The four massive spring sails are 60 feet across and drive two pairs of stones. The roundhouse contains milling artifacts and a collection of old photographs recording the mill's history. The mill is open from Easter to the end of October on Sundays and bank holidays from 2 pm to 6 pm. Telephone: 01342 843458.

FOREST GREEN AND EWHURST
– the old forest clearing

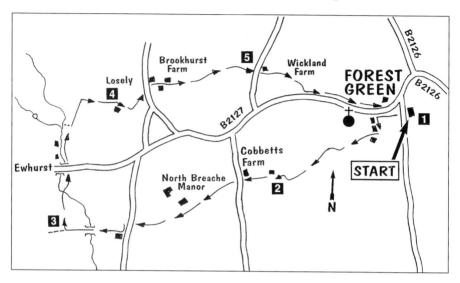

*T*his attractive field walk starts by the vast village green of Forest Green – said to be an early forest clearing dating from before Domesday. The route takes you over fields with splendid panoramic views across the surrounding countryside that surprisingly, is still thickly covered with trees. After passing North Breache Manor the route skirts the eastern edge of Ewhurst before returning through more pleasant farmland.

During early spring the wayside banks are dotted with primroses while a few weeks later the woods are carpeted by bluebells. Many rabbits, squirrels and hedgerow birds will be seen throughout the year. During winter after prolonged rain parts of this ramble can become rather churned up by farm animals so it is probably best left for drier weather.

THE WALK

1 With the Parrot behind you cross the green and turn left along a driveway signposted to Waterland Farm. Just before reaching a bungalow turn right at a stile by a field gate and continue along the right edge of two fields to soon enter a wonderful bluebell wood where you cross a bridge over a clear stream with banks lined by ferns and with alders (*see Walk 3*) dipping their roots into the water's edge. Keep ahead and go over a stile and press on along the left side of the field ahead, soon ignoring a stile. At the end of this field go over a stile beside a gate and continue onwards through another field. In 50 yards cross a stile in a hedge to your left to reach another stile. Cross this double stile over a brook and turn right along the right-hand field edge. Go over a stile under power cables and press on ahead. Cross two further stiles in quick succession in a band of oak woodland and continue ahead, passing a rather nice field maple. At another stile continue through a hazel coppice and press on up a slope. Go diagonally rightwards around the crest of the hill to meet a stile between two small peaceful ponds bordered by yellow flag and great reedmace (*see Walk 12*). It is nice to see that the landowner has newly planted young alder and dogwood here.

2 Press on up a slope to pass a bungalow and reach a road alongside the entrance to Cobbetts Farm. Cross the road and continue along the public footpath opposite. Plenty of rabbit activity goes on around here as the many burrows in the bank testify. At a stile maintain direction

STARTING POINT: At the Parrot public house in Horsham Road, Forest Green. This welcoming 17th century freehouse, set in 5 acres of grounds, is ideally situated opposite the village green and cricket pitch. Booking is recommended if you wish to dine at this popular pub. Telephone: 01306 621339.

HOW TO GET THERE: Forest Green lies just off the B2126 which runs between the A25 at Abinger Hammer and the A29 at Ockley, south of Dorking. On reaching the green turn into Horsham Road where you will find the Parrot public house.
    Carlone and Tillingbourne Buses serve the village

PARKING: Patrons of the Parrot may leave their cars in its car park while they walk (please ask first). There is alternative parking along Horsham Road.

LENGTH OF WALK: 4³/₄ miles. Map: OS Landranger 187 Dorking, Reigate and Crawley area (GR 124412).

along a field edge and a ditch. From here you will see lovely parkland vista with mature oaks standing majestically in the fields. Soon you pass the gardens to North Breache Manor and later a ha-ha with the house beyond. Press on ahead through another field alongside woodland. At a country lane turn left and soon go right alongside farm buildings on an enclosed path. Cross a stile alongside a gate and continue between fields to reach a substantial wooden bridge over a stream. Press on ahead along a well trodden path with an old boundary ditch and bank on your right.

3 Turn right at a distinct path on your right by a corner of a field and soon re-cross the stream that you crossed earlier. Maintain direction ahead on the main path through woodland that during spring is carpeted by bluebells. The call of the cuckoo, the most recognised bird call of all, will be heard between April and June on this ramble. By July or August the parent cuckoos will be gone, flying off back to Africa. The newly born juveniles will follow four or five weeks later. At a junction of paths, cross a stile ahead that is half hidden by a large holly bush and another in about 30 yards to continue on a fenced path to reach a road. Cross diagonally right to a public footpath and pass a couple of cottages. Press on over a couple of stiles and maintain direction along the field edge that mirrors the course of the stream. Ignore a stile on your left and continue to the far end of the field. Cross a stile and another in 20 yards where you now turn diagonally right over a field to a stile alongside a low barn.

4 Cross the stile and go through a gate to reach a driveway where you go rightwards along the drive. Here you will find an interesting variety of oak, ash and maple as well as hazel, brambles and dog rose lining the drive. Woody

The hazel coppice near Forest Green is coppiced every seven years for hurdle and rose arch making and the man seen here is one of the last hurdle makers in Surrey. The green wood is split before being skilfully woven and secured without nails or ties. Timber has always been too valuable a commodity for the extensive woodlands of the Weald to be left as waste. Since Neolithic times woodland has been managed with great care and where we now use iron, steel and concrete, the early builders used our indigenous hardwoods such as oak, beech and ash. Smaller household items and farm implements were made from coppiced hazel and ash.

*M*istletoe forms a part of our traditional Christmas decorations but its mystic associations go back much further than Christianity as there is some evidence that mistletoe was used in ancient druid rites. The plant is a parasite living on a variety of trees by extracting a part of the host's nutrients. The leaves, seeds and stems are highly poisonous and for centuries have been widely used in herbal medicine for the treatment of epilepsy, chorea and asthma. Kissing under a sprig of mistletoe is an ancient tradition that harks back to early fertility rites.

nightshade, a poisonous climbing plant, also grows here and during summer you will see the mauve and yellow flowers that resemble those of the potato to which it is related. During winter the bright red berries of black bryony, another poisonous climber, will be seen adorning the brambles like strings of shiny beads. When a road is reached turn left and in 50 yards turn right on a public footpath along the drive to Brookhurst Farm. Continue ahead along the right side of a large barn and pass through the left of two gates. Go ahead down a slope and through a gap in a line of trees to cross a second field to a stile by the edge of woodland which is to the left of the large green barn ahead. Cross the stile and continue ahead on a farm track and soon pass a pond. At a five bar gate cross another stile and continue along the farm track.

5 When a road is reached turn right and in 20 yards turn leftwards on a path. Cross a stile and continue along the right-hand field edge. The views across to Leith Hill are quite breathtaking. At the end of the field go right over a stile to reach a road. Turn left along the road where soon after crossing a stream the wide expanse of the green at Forest Green is met. A little further along the green you come to the Parrot and the end of the walk.

PLACE OF INTEREST NEARBY
Dorking Museum, housed in a former foundry, has a large display of local history including paintings, prints and photographs. It is situated in West Street, Dorking. Telephone: 01306 876591.

HANKLEY COMMON AND THURSLEY NATURE RESERVE

– *a wilder side of Surrey*

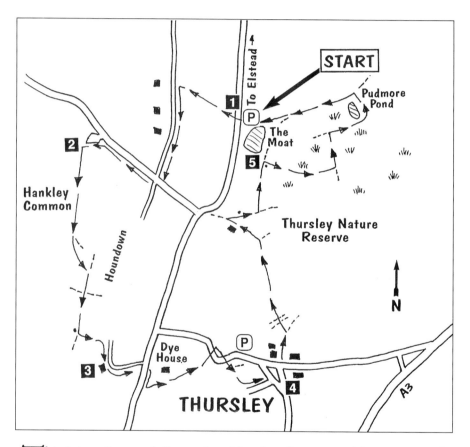

*T*his interesting and diverse heathland walk starts at The Moat pond – an oasis amongst the gorse and heather of Thursley Nature Reserve. The route soon continues along the top of a high ridge across the wilder reaches of Hankley Common where on a warm summer's day you may be rewarded with the sight of kestrels hovering seemingly motionless above the heather in their quest for prey.

At the turning point of the walk the route passes old cottages in Thursley where time seems to have stood still for centuries. The path then returns across Thursley Nature Reserve where boardwalks take you through the nationally important and rare bog habitat. During summer over 20 species of dragonfly can be seen hunting among the many pools. The wet and dry heath is also the home of the silver studded butterfly, Dartford warbler, marsh orchids and myriads of tiny sundew that live on the peaty soil.

THE WALK

1 Go back to the entrance of The Moat car park and cross the road diagonally right to a footpath opposite. Press on along this path soon going through wrought iron gates. When a lane is met by the ornate gates of Elstead Manor, turn left. This very quiet lane, no more than a cart track, leads you through woodland that is alive with bird song. At a road junction turn right along an uphill road. Before the crest of the hill is reached turn left and enter a car park where you continue to the far end of the car park and press on up steps.

2 At the top turn left along a broad track that keeps to the top of the ridge. This is a great vantage point for viewing kestrels and on a

STARTING POINT: This is the one walk that does not start at or even near a pub or place for refreshment so take a picnic. The Moat pond is the ideal place for this.

HOW TO GET THERE: From Guildford take the A3 and travel south for 3 miles then take the B3001 to Elstead. Turn left at the small village green in Elstead and in 1¼ miles The Moat car park will be found on your left.

Stagecoach Hants & Surrey buses serve the area.

PARKING: There is a large car park alongside The Moat and only on the busiest day will a parking spot be scarce.

LENGTH OF WALK: 5¼ miles. Map: OS Landranger 186 Aldershot, Guildford and surrounding area (GR 899416).

fine day I like to sit here for a while just taking in the stillness. Down on the valley floor is the base camp of the army units that train here on this difficult terrain so just occasionally that stillness is shattered. Disregard crossing paths and at a fork stay ahead on the right fork. Soon at a junction of tracks turn right down a gully to the valley floor. Press on over a crossing track at the bottom and continue up the other side. At the top maintain direction along the main track and soon after going up a deeply rutted gully you go forward to meet a junction of tracks by a post. Turn left here and follow a path through pine trees. At a crossing track under power cables continue ahead and soon go slightly left as the way is joined by another path from your right. Within yards the path goes downhill to meet a track. Turn right along this track that very soon brings you to a lane by a house with a picturesque garden.

3 Continue forwards along the lane as it goes uphill through trees to soon meet a road. Turn right along the road and 30 yards after passing the entrance to Dye House turn left on a pretty footpath that in spring is lined with primroses and bluebells. After crossing a small stream the path leads you over a second stream and ends at a driveway. Turn left along the drive to meet a road by pretty cottages. Turn right along the road and very soon take a footpath on your right. In 10 yards turn right again and continue up a gully. This path cut into the side of a hill eventually brings you to a road named The Lane where, after passing old cottages you find yourself at Thursley village green with its splendid old acacia trees.

4 Continue ahead alongside the road for a few yards and then turn right on a bridleway alongside Vean Cottage. In 25 yards after passing a nature reserve sign turn left on a path and go over two crossing tracks in quick succession. When a field

The sundew is different from most English plants in that it is insectivorous. The small rosette of long stalked leaves have reddish sticky hairs around the margins that attract insects. Once the insect is trapped by these hairs the leaf curls inwards and completely encloses the victim which is then digested and absorbed. The carnivorous nature of this plant is probably an adaptation to its nutrient poor habitat.

The many dragonflies seen flying around the pools on this ramble during summer started life as nymphs living underwater for anything up to five years and breathing through gills as fish do. When they reach adulthood they climb up a reed stem and discard their outer skin as in this picture. The fully developed adult, now with transparent veined wings, will live for only one further year. Throughout their entire life they are ferocious carnivores living on flies, mosquitoes and gnats.

is spotted through the trees ahead, you should take a right fork. This path skirts Thursley Nature Reserve over to your right and shadows the field and bridleway to your left. At the far corner of the field bear leftwards and pass an old barn to reach a cottage via a farm track. Some 30 yards after passing the cottage turn sharply right along a bridleway and soon pass a gate and information cairn. In 100 yards turn left on a broad sandy bridleway.

5 Keep ahead now and after $\frac{1}{3}$ mile look out for a narrow path on your right by a pine tree and short post. Turn right here and within yards you meet the first of many boardwalks that lead you through the bog. This rare habitat is a joy during summer and many dragonflies will be seen. A closer inspection of the pool edges will reveal myriads of tiny sundew. Easier to spot are the marsh orchids and cotton grass. At a T-junction, turn left and continue through a stand of Scots pine. Once out of the trees bear left on a narrow path that again leads you to a boardwalk where you maintain direction through a second stand of pine. After passing a dragonfly information board a T-junction is met where you should turn right. Eventually, when this narrow path meets a T-junction with a broad track, turn left. Continue along this broad track that again, under close inspection will reveal hundreds of tiny sundew plants awaiting unwary insects. At a fork ignore the left path and soon The Moat pond with its waterfowl and unique colony of water spiders is reached.

PLACE OF INTEREST NEARBY

Witley Common Information Centre is a fragment of the lowland heath that once covered much of southern England. There are guided walks along nature trails through different habitats throughout the year. The information centre explains the importance of heathland to wildlife and its management. There is a small shop where tea, coffee and soft drinks can be bought and picnic tables are available. The information centre is open from the end of March to the end of October. Opening days are Mondays to Thursdays from 11 am to 4 pm and Saturdays, Sundays and bank holidays from 11 am to 5 pm. The centre is 1 mile south-west of Milford off the A286. Telephone: 01428 683207.

WALK 19

CHIDDINGFOLD, HAZEL BRIDGE AND BOTANY BAY

– field paths and glorious groves

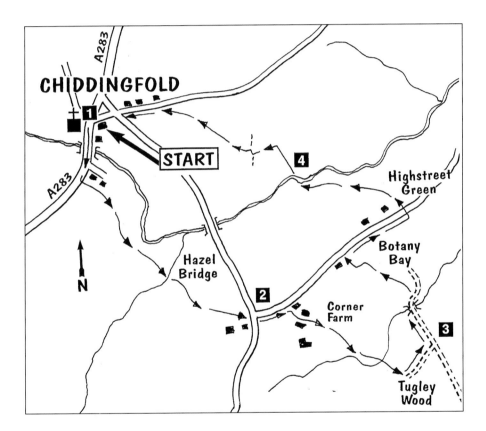

*T*his field path and woodland walk is excellent at any time of the year but must surely be at its best in spring when primroses, bluebells and especially wood anemones blanket the woodland floor. The woods around here were for centuries the centre of the glass making industry where plentiful quantities of charcoal, sand and water power provided the main ingredients. The sound of this industry has long departed and the woods are now alive with birdsong.

89

The route traverses a couple of valleys where the streams that made this area so productive tumble along the valley floors. There are plenty of hedgerow and woodland birds to see and hear as well as a wealth of spring flowers.

THE WALK

1 With your back to the Crown Inn turn left and walk alongside the main A283. Cross the infant river Arun and soon after passing a road named Turners Mead go left on an enclosed footpath. After passing the rear of gardens cross a stile and continue along the right side of a field by a line of mature oaks. Go over a stile and enter a band of bluebell wood. Cross another stile where you now turn left and continue along the left-hand field edge. At yet another stile you should continue ahead through woodland where the path soon goes down steps to meet a stream running through a sheltered valley where mosses and ferns appreciate the shelter and humidity. A summer visitor to this moist habitat is the rather plain looking nightingale whose song has inspired so many poets. Go over two small bridges and climb a rise to a stile which you

PARKING: At the Crown Inn alongside the village green at Chiddingfold. The Crown Inn is thought to have been built in 1285 and is said to be the oldest inn remaining in Surrey, although it does not appear in records until the 14th century. Food from the bar, vegetarian and à la carte menus is served between 12 noon and 2.30 pm and 7 pm to 9.30 pm every day. Telephone: 01428 682255.

HOW TO GET THERE: From the A3 south of Guildford take the road into Milford from where you should travel south for 4 miles on the A283. The Crown Inn is alongside the village green to your left.

Stagecoach Buses serve the area.

PARKING: Patrons of the Crown Inn may use the car park while they walk (please ask first). There is alternative parking along the side of the green.

LENGTH OF WALK: 4 miles. Map: OS Landranger 186 Aldershot, Guildford and surrounding area (GR 961355).

cross. Continue ahead along the right-hand field edge and at the end of the field go immediately left into another field. Keep to the right-hand side and follow a ditch and bank on your right where the scrub is adorned by dog roses. Watch your footing as moles and rabbits abound here. At the end of this field cross a stile and go forward to a drive where you turn left to reach a road.

2 Continue ahead along the road named High Street Green and 20 yards after passing the entrance to Follies Farm go right on a signposted footpath. Press on along a well manicured broad grass strip to reach a farm track and two barns. Continue along a driveway through an avenue of ornamental trees. At the end of the drive press on ahead along another well manicured strip of grass that during spring boasts hundreds of minute narcissi. Keep ahead along the edge of these magnificent and well kept gardens. Ignore a stile to your left by a field and maintain direction to enter a more natural woodland scene. Continue along this path bordered by the graceful pendulous sedge that during June and July sends up flowering spikes as high as 1.5 m. After crossing a stream continue ahead up a rise and at an indistinct T-junction bear left. Soon a forestry track is reached where you bear left and continue along it.

3 At a T-junction with another forestry track turn left. Soon you pass a clearing on your left where a sea of the tall wild oat grass waves in the breeze. Roe deer (*see Walk 15*) frequent this part of the forest and on quiet days it is possible to see one or two. About 100 yards after the track crosses a stream and halfway round a right-hand bend look out for a small path going off to the left. Proceed along this rising narrow path through a peaceful area of woodland called

The wood anemone, pictured here in March and also known as the wind flower, is a member of the buttercup family. It is an early spring flower growing in large clumps and emerges from an underground stem called a rhizome. The white flowers, sometimes tinged with pink are pollinated by beetles and bees which welcome an early start to the year. The plant dies back in early summer. At one time these pretty plants were used in herbal medicine but are now out of favour due to the rather harsh and irritating sap they produce.

Botany Bay. A good indication of the dampness and humidity of this woodland are the mosses and ferns growing here. Look closely at the moss-covered tree stumps and you will see the minute candle snuff fungus. Follow the waymarked path until it eventually reaches a road alongside a bungalow. Turn right along the road and ignore a footpath soon reached on your left. About 30 yards after passing the entrance to a house named Deerfold go leftwards on a footpath that takes you through oak woodland that is carpeted by wood anemones during spring. One of the birds I spotted here was the lively little willow tit whose name is rather misleading as it is a creature of damp oak woodland and hedgerows. Ignore any side paths and stay on the main path as it goes down to the valley floor to reach the river Arun.

4 Cross the wooden bridge and go leftwards to soon reach a field. Turn right here and press on up the right-hand field edge lined with hazel and dog roses. At the top of the field turn left with a hedge on your right. Watch out for a gap with a small planked bridge by a marker post. Go through the hedge here and continue diagonally leftwards across the corner of the field to reach a marker post by a woodland strip. Continue in the same direction through the trees and cross a stile. Maintain direction ahead over another field to a further ribbon of trees where you cross a small stream. Continue ahead over a field and cross a stile at the far side where you press on to meet a stile by a house. Turn left here and walk along the lane where soon after passing Chiddingfold Post Office the village green is met. A few yards further and the Crown Inn and the end of the walk are reached.

PLACES OF INTEREST NEARBY
Ramster Gardens were laid out in 1904 and contain 20 acres of woodland, bog and flowering shrub garden. The privately owned gardens include a pretty lake. Open from mid April to mid July from 11 am to 5.30 pm. The gardens are 1 mile south of Chiddingfold off the A283. Telephone: 01428 654167.

Winkworth Arboretum, owned by the National Trust, can be found at Godalming, just north of Chiddingfold. In addition to the fine collection of shrubs and trees, there is also a lake, home to plenty of birdlife. Telephone: 01483 208477.

ALFOLD AND SIDNEY WOOD

– *ancient Wealden forest*

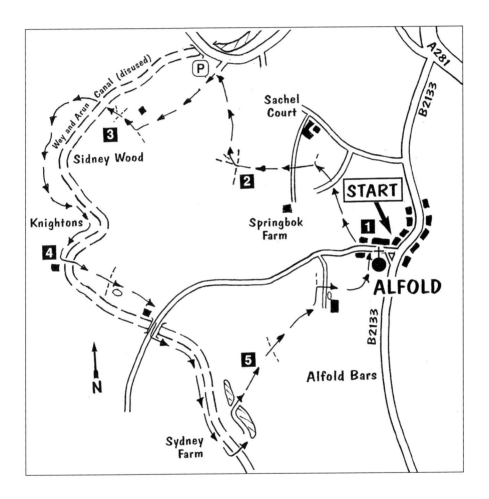

*T*his superb walk starts in the Arcadian village of Alfold close to the Sussex border. After crossing farmland the route takes you through Sidney Wood named after the de Sydenie family of Alfold. Interestingly, Sydney in Australia is named after the same family. This wonderful indigenous forest was an important centre of glass making between the

13th and 17th centuries and the route passes the indistinct remains of Knightons Glasshouse.

Many birds will be seen and heard as you walk through peaceful woodland which is carpeted by bluebells and wood anemones during the spring months. For some of the way the route follows the towpath of the now disused Wey and Arun Canal that, together with the Wey Navigation, created a link from the river Thames to the south coast. The return to Alfold is via pretty field paths.

THE WALK

1 With your back to the Crown pub walk rightwards along the pretty lane and ignore a public footpath at the drive to Linden Farm. Soon after passing a bungalow on your right, turn right on a public footpath. Maintain direction over three stiles to reach a large field. Go ahead here to a fourth stile by a farm track. Cross the farm drive and press on ahead to yet another stile. Turn leftwards here and carry on to a stile to the left of a small barn. Cross this stile and another in 10 yards and continue

STARTING POINT: At the Crown public house in Loxwood Road, Alfold. This 16th century establishment, owned by the Morland Brewery, is a typical village pub and is just a stone's throw from the beautiful church of St Nicholas. This is a small village pub and there are no facilities for children. Telephone: 01403 752216.

HOW TO GET THERE: Alfold is approximately 8 miles south of Guildford off the A281. Turn onto the B2133 at Alfold Cross and in ½ mile the Crown public house will be seen on your right alongside the tiny village green.

Tillingbourne Buses serve the village

PARKING: Ramblers using the Crown may, with prior permission, leave their cars in the pub car park while they walk. Alternative parking is at the roadside on the B2133.

LENGTH OF WALK: 5 miles. Map: OS Landranger 186 Aldershot, Guildford and surrounding area (GR 038340).

along a field edge to reach woodland ahead. Enter the woodland where in spring you will see clumps of primroses among the carpets of bluebells and wood anemones (*see Walk 19*). When another path is met in a few yards keep ahead.

2 At a broad crossing track go forward for 30 yards and then bear right on a narrower path between the trees. In 20 yards ignore a left fork and press on to cross a stile at a field edge. Continue ahead along the field edge to reach another stile where you re-enter the woodland. When this pretty path swings left away from the field keep right at a fork and soon a wide forestry track is reached. Turn leftwards along this track and soon pass a car park on your right. Handy picnic tables can be found at the end of the car park. Press on along the broad track and turn right when a T-junction is reached. Many chaffinches will be seen going about their daily business among the trees here as well as larger birds such as jays and green woodpeckers.

*A*sh wood is third in economic importance after oak and beech. 300 years ago John Evelyn wrote that 'the farmer cannot be without ash for his carts, ladders and other tackling, from the pike, spear and bow, to the plough'. Today it still has many uses which include handles for axes and garden tools, oars, snooker cues and surprisingly, in the manufacture of Morgan motorcars. In folklore it was said to have magical powers and a circle of ash twigs laid around you as you slept formed a barrier from adders, a much more common snake in those days. Its bark was brewed and was given as a cure for anything from sore throats to the plague. More recently it has been found that the bark contains quinine, a drug once used to treat malaria.

3 When this forestry track bends sharply left at a junction of tracks with a house and tennis court visible on your right you should continue ahead on a narrower track between trees. At a distinct fork in the track bear left where you soon pass a welcome wooden seat. Soon you cross the remains of the Wey and Arun Canal where you maintain direction ahead. Keep to the main track at all times as it winds its way through the magnificent woodland. Later, a few yards past a second seat the towpath of the disused canal is reached. During late summer and autumn look out for the fungi that thrive on the rotting vegetation this woodland offers. Continue rightwards along the towpath until you reach a forestry track by a large house.

4 Turn left along this track and when another forestry track is met, press on ahead. The route soon passes a small woodland pool that is an oasis for dragonflies (*see Walk 18*). Eventually go through a gate to pass a house and reach a country lane. Turn right along the lane and after 30 yards or so turn left to rejoin the canal bank. During spring you should see one or two early purple orchids along this pleasant path. After walking for around 1/2 mile ignore a stile on your right but 100 yards later turn left over a stile and cross a field to another stile by a seat and fingerpost. Turn left here and continue alongside a small lake where during spring there is a wonderful array of bluebells, primroses and cuckoo flowers. Soon after crossing a small planked bridge turn right over a causeway and cross a stile in the field edge ahead.

5 Maintain direction ahead and cross another stile tucked away in the far corner. Press on along the left field edge to reach a fingerpost by a field gate. Ignore the bridleway to your left and continue through the field gate ahead. Cross the field diagonally half left to a further fingerpost alongside another field gate. Press on through this gate and go forward to the far corner of the field to a stile. Go over this stile and continue along a field edge with a drive and ornamental pond to your right. Soon, go right over a stile and cross two driveways to a further stile opposite. Cross this and go ahead along the right-hand field edge. Follow the waymarked signs over another four stiles to reach a small graveyard. Continue through the graveyard to soon reach a road where you now turn right and retrace your steps back to the Crown public house and the end of the walk.

PLACE OF INTEREST NEARBY
The Countryways Experience was once a working farm. It is now a farming museum and a place where all the family can enjoy an afternoon or a day out. Children can feed most of the small animals, including lambs, goats and piglets. There are pony and tractor rides plus indoor and outdoor play areas. For those of us a little older there are woodland walks, a Victorian walled garden, farm shop and tearoom. No dogs are allowed – except guide dogs. From the A281 at Alfold Cross 8 miles south of Guildford follow the tourist signs. Telephone: 01403 753589.